Nick Vandome

macOS

for all Macs (iMac, Mac mini, Mac Pro and MacBook)
Illustrated using macOS Ventura

In easy steps is an imprint of In Easy Steps Limited
16 Hamilton Terrace · Holly Walk · Leamington Spa
Warwickshire · United Kingdom · CV32 4LY
www.ineasysteps.com

Notice of Liability
Every effort has been made to ensure that this book contains accurate
and current information. However, In Easy Steps Limited and the
author shall not be liable for any loss or damage suffered by readers
as a result of any information contained herein.

Trademarks
OS X® and macOS® are registered trademarks of Apple Computer
Inc. All other trademarks are acknowledged as belonging to their
respective companies.

In Easy Steps Limited supports The Forest Stewardship Council (FSC),
the leading international forest certification organization. All our titles
that are printed on Greenpeace approved FSC certified paper carry the
FSC logo.

MIX
Paper from
responsible sources
FSC® C020837

FSC
www.fsc.org

Printed and bound in the United Kingdom

ISBN 978-1-84078-983-6

Contents

1 Introducing macOS

macOS is the operating system from Apple, for its range of desktop and laptop computers. This chapter introduces macOS, showing how to install it and become familiar with the user interface and some of the features needed to get up and running.

About macOS Ventura

macOS Ventura is the latest major version of the operating system (*released in 2022*) for Apple computers: the iMac, iMac Pro, MacBook Air, MacBook Pro, Mac mini, Mac Studio and Mac Pro. It is the first version of the operating system to have the "13" designation after various other macOS version numbers. macOS is still based on the UNIX programming language, which is a very stable and secure operating environment, and this ensures that macOS is secure, user-friendly and stylish.

macOS Ventura continues the functionality of several of its Mac operating system predecessors, including using some of the features that are available on Apple's mobile devices such as the iPad and the iPhone – for example, Multitasking Gestures.

Some of the new and updated features of macOS Ventura are:

- **Stage Manager**. This is an organization feature that minimizes open apps at the side of the screen so that they can be accessed quickly, with one app being made the currently-active one, in the center of the screen.

- **System Settings**. What was previously known as System Preferences on Mac computers has been redesigned as System Settings, to make the feature more similar to the versions on iPhones and iPads.

- **Undo Send for iMessages and emails**. It is now possible to retrieve an iMessage text message or an email using the **Undo Send** feature, if an item has been sent in error or contains mistakes. It is also possible to edit iMessages.

- **Shared iCloud Photo Library**. This enables greater flexibility for sharing photos with family and friends, using the online backup and sharing feature, iCloud.

UNIX is an operating system that has traditionally been used for large commercial mainframe computers. It is renowned for its stability and ability to be used within different computing environments.

The Apple Pencil can be used on some Mac computers with macOS to perform tasks such as drawing and sketching, in compatible apps, and marking up screenshots and PDF documents.

Installing macOS Ventura

When it comes to installing macOS Ventura you do not need to worry about an installation CD or DVD; it can be downloaded and installed directly from the online App Store. New Macs will have macOS Ventura installed. The following range is compatible with macOS Ventura and can be upgraded with it, directly from the App Store:

- iMac (2017 or newer).

- iMac Pro (all models).

- MacBook (2017).

- MacBook Pro (2017 or newer).

- MacBook Air (2018 or newer).

- Mac mini (2018 or newer).

- Mac Pro (2019 or newer).

If you want to install macOS Ventura on an existing Mac, you will need to have the minimum requirements of:

- 2GB of memory.

- 12.5GB of available storage for installation.

If your Mac meets these requirements, you can download and install macOS Ventura, for free, as follows:

1 Click on this icon on the Dock to access the App Store (or select **Software Update**; see the second Hot tip)

App Store

2 Locate the **macOS Ventura** icon using the App Store Search box

macOS Ventura
Utilities
GET

3 Click on the **Get** button and follow the installation instructions

GET

Don't forget

macOS Ventura is the latest version of the Mac operating system at the time of printing. It contains a number of enhancements to make the operating system faster and more reliable than ever.

Hot tip

For details about using the Dock, see pages 24-31.

Hot tip

To check your computer's software version, access **System Settings > General > Software Update**.

The macOS Environment

The first most noticeable element about macOS is its elegant user interface. This has been designed to create a user-friendly graphic overlay to the UNIX operating system at the heart of macOS, and it is a combination of rich colors and sharp, original graphics. The main elements that make up the initial macOS environment are:

Apple menu   Menu bar   Windows   Menu bar icons

The Dock   Desktop

Hot tip

The Dock is designed to help make organizing and opening items as quick and easy as possible. For a detailed look at the Dock, see Chapter 2.

Don't forget

Many of the behind-the-scenes features of macOS are aimed at saving power on your Mac. These include timer-coalescing technologies for saving processing and battery power; features for saving energy when apps are not being used; power-saving features in Safari for ignoring additional content provided by web page plug-ins; and memory compression to make your Mac quicker and more responsive.

The **Apple menu** is standardized throughout macOS, regardless of the app in use.

Menus

Menus in macOS contain commands for the operating system and any relevant apps. If there is an arrow next to a command, it means there are subsequent options for the item. Some menus also incorporate the same transparency as the sidebar so that the background shows through.

Transparency

One feature in macOS is that the sidebar and toolbars in certain apps are transparent so that you can see some of the Desktop behind it. This also helps the uppermost window blend in with the background.

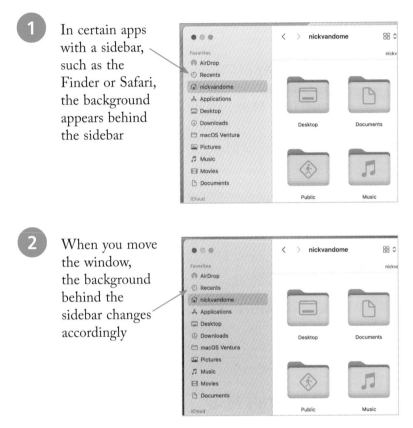

1 In certain apps with a sidebar, such as the Finder or Safari, the background appears behind the sidebar

2 When you move the window, the background behind the sidebar changes accordingly

Window control buttons

These appear in any open macOS window and can be used to manipulate the window. They include a full-screen option. Use the window buttons to, from left to right: close a window, minimize a window, or access full-screen mode (if available).

If an app has full-screen functionality, click on this button to return to standard view:

If an option is gray, it means it is not available; i.e. the screen cannot be maximized.

Don't forget

The red window button is used to close a window, and in some cases – such as with Notes, Reminders and Calendar – it also closes the app. The amber button is used to minimize a window so that it appears at the right-hand side of the Dock.

About This Mac

When you buy a new Mac, you will almost certainly check the technical specifications before you make a purchase. Once you have your Mac, there will be times when you will want to view these specifications again, such as the version of macOS in use or the amount of system storage. This can be done through the **About This Mac** option, which can be accessed from the Apple menu. To do this:

1 Click on the **Apple menu** button and click on the **About This Mac** option

2 Details about your Mac are displayed

Don't forget

About This Mac information can also be viewed in **System Settings** > **General** > **About**.

3 Click on the **More Info...** button to view full details about the hardware and software on your Mac

4 The **About This Mac** details are displayed in the **System Settings** app

12

5 Scroll up the panel to view all of the related items

For more information about software updates, see page 181.

6 Click on the **Display Settings...** button in Step 5 to view details of the screen display. Drag this slider to adjust the screen brightness

Drag the **Automatically adjust brightness** button **On** in Step 6 to enable the screen brightness to change, depending on the ambient lighting.

13

7 Click on the **Storage Settings...** button in Step 5 to view the storage details for your Mac, including how content is stored in the iCloud online storage facility

About System Settings

macOS has a wide range of options for customizing and configuring the way that your Mac operates. These are located within the **System Settings** section. To access this:

Don't forget

For more detailed information about the Dock, see Chapter 2.

1 Click on this button on the Dock (the bar of icons that appears along the bottom of the screen), or access it from the **Applications** folder

2 All of the categories are shown in the left-hand sidebar of the **System Settings** window

Don't forget

For a detailed look at System Settings, see pages 32-33.

3 Click on a category in the left-hand sidebar to open its options in the main **System Settings** window. Each item will have a number of options for customization

Search Options

Finding items on a Mac or on the web is an important part of everyday computing, and with macOS there are a number of options for doing this.

Siri

Siri is Apple's digital voice assistant that can search for items using speech. It has been available on Apple's mobile devices using iOS and iPadOS for a number of years, and with macOS it is available on Macs and MacBooks. See pages 17-19 for more details about setting up and using Siri.

Spotlight search

Spotlight is the dedicated search app for macOS. It can be used over all the files on your Mac and the internet. To use Spotlight:

1 Click on this icon at the right of the Apple Menu bar

2 Click in the **Spotlight Search** box

3 Enter a keyword or phrase for which you want to search

4 The top hits from within your apps, and the web, are shown in the left-hand panel. Click on an item to view its details

See pages 17-19 for more details about setting up and using Siri.

It is possible to find photos directly in Spotlight search. To do this, enter the search word or phrase, followed by "photos". The results will be displayed in the **Spotlight Search** panel. The results can be from the web and your own apps.

15

Spotlight starts searching for items as soon as you start typing a word. So, don't worry if some of the first results look inappropriate, as these will disappear once you have finished typing the full word.

...cont'd

5 For items linked to apps on your Mac, click on an item to view the information in the relevant app

6 For items from the web, click on an item to view the related web page(s)

Don't forget

Click on a folder in Step 7 to open it directly in the Finder.

7 For other locations within your Mac, click on an item to see the details in the main window

8 Below the **Related Searches** heading are options for searching the web or in your Mac's Finder

Finder search

This is the Search box in the top right-hand corner of the Finder and can be used to search for items within it. See page 71 for details about using Finder search.

Using Siri

Siri is the digital voice assistant that can be used to vocally search for a wide range of items from your Mac and the web. Also, the results can be managed in innovative ways so that keeping up-to-date is easier than ever.

Setting up Siri

To set up and start using Siri:

1 Open **System Settings** and click on the **Siri & Spotlight** tab

2 Drag the **Ask Siri** button **On**

Siri & Spotlight

Ask Siri	
Siri helps you get things done, just by asking. Dictate a note, check the weather, and more.	

Keyboard shortcut	Hold Command Space ⇕
Language	English (United States) ⇕
Siri voice	American (Voice 2) Select...
Siri history	Delete Siri & Dictation History...
	Siri Suggestions & Privacy... Siri Responses...

3 Make selections here for how Siri operates, including language and the voice used by Siri

4 Click on the **Siri** icon on the Dock or in the Menu bar to open Siri

5 The Siri window opens, ready for use

Mon 12:20 PM

Hot tip

An internal or external microphone is required in order to ask Siri questions.

Searching with Siri

Siri can respond to most requests, including playing a music track, checking the weather, opening photos, and adding calendar events. It is also possible to ask questions of Siri while you are working on another document.

Siri can search for a vast range of items, from your Mac or the web. Some useful Siri functions include:

Opening apps

Apps can be opened by Siri, with a simple "open" command:

Working with apps

Siri can also be used to add content to certain apps, such as adding an event to the calendar, adding a reminder, or creating a new note and adding content to it. This is done by asking Siri to create a new note, with the required text:

Hot tip

To display your own questions to Siri on the screen, access **System Settings** > **Siri & Spotlight**. Click on the **Siri Responses** button and drag the **Always show speech** option **On**.

General information

Siri can be used to display a wide range of general information. Make an enquiry and see what Siri displays. In a lot of instances there will be links to relevant websites, such as Wikipedia.

Move the cursor over the Siri search results and click on the cross in the top left-hand corner of the Siri window to close it.

Weather forecasts

Siri can also provide weather forecasts for locations around the world. It can also display local information (if **Location Services** is turned **On**), such as local restaurants or movies that are playing nearby.

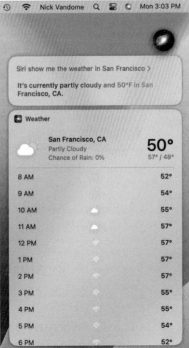

Accessibility

In all areas of computing it is important to give as many people as possible access to the system. This includes users with visual impairments and also people who have problems using the mouse and keyboard. In macOS this is achieved through the functions of the **Accessibility** section of **System Settings**. To use these:

Don't forget

Another option in the **Accessibility** window is for **Switch Control**, which enables a Mac to be controlled by a variety of devices including the mouse, keypad and gamepad devices.

Don't forget

Experiment with the **VoiceOver** function, if only to see how it operates. This will give you a better idea of how visually-impaired users access information on a computer.

1 Click on the **Accessibility** tab in the left-hand sidebar of **System Settings**

Accessibility

2 Click on the **Display** option to change the settings for display colors and contrast, and to increase the cursor size

Accessibility

Vision
- VoiceOver
- Zoom
- Display
- Spoken Content
- Descriptions

Hearing
- Audio
- RTT
- Captions

Motor
- Voice Control
- Keyboard
- Pointer Control

3 Click on the **Zoom** option to change the settings for zooming in on the screen

4 Click on the **VoiceOver** option to enable VoiceOver, which provides a spoken description of what is on the screen

5 Click on the **Audio** option to select an on-screen flash for alerts, and settings for how sound is played

6 Click on the **Keyboard** option to access settings for customizing the keyboard

7 Click on the **Pointer Control** option to access settings for customizing the mouse and trackpad

The Spoken Word

macOS not only has numerous apps for adding text to documents, emails and messages; it also has a **Dictation** function so that you can speak what you want to appear on screen. To set up and use the **Dictation** feature:

1 Click on the **Keyboard** tab in **System Settings**

2 By default, the **Dictation** option is **Off**. Drag the button **On** to enable Dictation

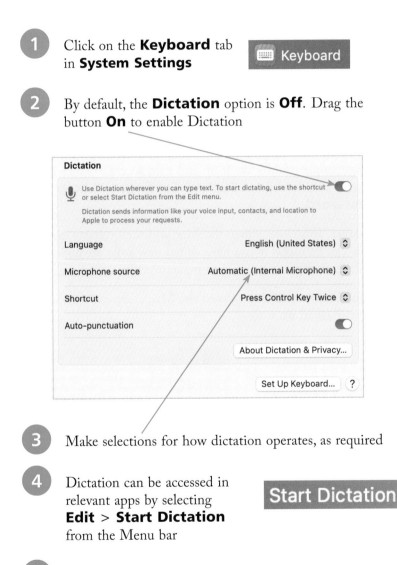

Dictation

🎤 Use Dictation wherever you can type text. To start dictating, use the shortcut or select Start Dictation from the Edit menu.

Dictation sends information like your voice input, contacts, and location to Apple to process your requests.

Language	English (United States) ⌄
Microphone source	Automatic (Internal Microphone) ⌄
Shortcut	Press Control Key Twice ⌄
Auto-punctuation	🔵

About Dictation & Privacy...

Set Up Keyboard... ?

3 Make selections for how dictation operates, as required

4 Dictation can be accessed in relevant apps by selecting **Edit** > **Start Dictation** from the Menu bar

5 Start talking when the microphone icon appears. Click **Done** when you have finished recording your text

Hot tip

Punctuation can be added with the **Dictation** function, by speaking commands such as "comma" or "question mark". These will then be converted into the appropriate symbols.

Don't forget

Dictation settings can also be found in **System Settings** > **Accessibility** – see Step 8 on the previous page.

Shutting Down

The Apple menu (which can be accessed by clicking on the Apple icon in the top-left corner of the Desktop, or any subsequent macOS window) is standardized in macOS. This means that it has the same options regardless of the app in which you are working. This has a number of advantages, not least being the fact that it makes it easier to shut down your Mac. When shutting down, there are three options that can be selected:

- **Sleep.** This puts the Mac into hibernation mode; i.e. the screen goes blank and the hard drive becomes inactive. This state is maintained until the mouse is moved or a key is pressed on the keyboard. This then wakes up the Mac and it is ready to continue work. It is a good idea to add a login password for accessing the Mac when it wakes up, otherwise other people could wake it up and gain access to it. To add a login password, go to **System Settings** > **Login Password**.

- **Restart.** This closes down the Mac and then restarts it again. This can be useful if you have added new software and your computer requires a restart to make it active.

- **Shut Down.** This closes down the Mac completely once you have finished working.

When shutting down, make sure you have saved all of your open documents, although macOS will prompt you to do this if you have forgotten.

If a password is added, the Lock screen will appear whenever the Mac is woken from sleep, and the password will be required to unlock it.

Users of the Apple Watch can unlock their Mac running macOS, without a password.

macOS has a resuming feature, where the Mac opens up in the same state as when it was shut down. See page 56 for details.

Click here to access the **Apple menu**

Click here to access one of the shutdown options

🍎	**Finder**	File	Edit	View

About This Mac

System Settings...
App Store...

Recent Items ›

Force Quit... ⌥⌘⊘

Sleep
Restart...
Shut Down...

Lock Screen ⌃⌘Q
Log Out Nick Vandome... ⇧⌘Q

2 Getting Up and Running

This chapter looks at some of the essential features of macOS. These include the Dock for organizing and accessing all the elements of your Mac computer; System Settings for the way your Mac looks and operates; and options for arranging folders and files and your Mac workspace. It also details the online service – iCloud – for sharing digital content, including the Family Sharing feature for sharing with family members.

Introducing the Dock

The Dock is one of the main organizational elements of macOS. Its main function is to help organize and access apps, folders and files. In addition, with its background and icons, it also makes an aesthetically-pleasing addition to the Desktop. The main things to remember about the Dock are:

- It is divided into two: apps go on the left of the dividing line; all other items, and open apps, go on the right.

- It can be customized in several different ways.

By default, the Dock appears at the bottom of the screen:

Apps go here   Dividing line   Minimized open items

By default, the two icons to the right of the dividing line are:

Downloads. This is for items that you have downloaded from the web. The items can be accessed from here, and opened or run.

Trash. This is where items can be dragged to if you want to remove them. It can also be used to eject removable devices, such as flashdrives, by dragging the device's icon over the Trash icon. It cannot be removed from the Dock.

Don't forget

The Dock is always displayed as a line of icons, but this can be orientated either vertically or horizontally.

Hot tip

The **Downloads** icon can be displayed as a folder or a Stack. To set this, **Ctrl + click** on the **Downloads** icon and select either **Folder** or **Stack** under the **Display as** option.

Apps on the Dock

Opening apps

When you open apps, they appear on the Dock and can be worked with within the Dock environment.

 Click once on an app to open it (either on the Dock, in the Finder Applications folder or the Launchpad). Once an app has been opened, it is displayed on the Dock with a dot below it

 When an open app is minimized, it is displayed to the right of the dividing line

 Click on an icon to the right of the dividing line to maximize it: it disappears from the right-hand side of the Dock and displays at full size

 If a window is minimized by clicking on this button, it goes back to the right-hand side of the dividing line on the Dock

 Press and hold below an open app to view the available windows for the app (this will differ for individual apps, as some operate by using a single window)

 To close an open app, press and hold on the black dot below its icon on the Dock and click on the **Quit** button (or select its name on the Menu bar and select **Quit**)

Hot tip

Items on the Dock can be opened by clicking on them once, rather than having to double-click them. Once they have been accessed, the icon bobs up and down until the item is available.

Don't forget

Apps can be opened from the Dock, the Finder or the Launchpad. The Finder is covered in detail in Chapter 3, and see pages 92-93 for more on the Launchpad.

Don't forget

Some apps (such as Notes, Reminders and Calendar) will close when the active window is closed. Others (such as Pages, Keynote and Numbers) will remain open even if all of the windows are closed: recently-accessed documents will be displayed as in the context menu in Step 5.

Applying Dock Settings

As with most elements of macOS, the Dock can be modified in numerous ways. This can affect both the appearance of the Dock and the way it operates. To set Dock settings:

1 Select **System Settings > Desktop & Dock**

2 The Dock settings allow you to change its size, orientation, the way icons appear with magnification, and effects for when items are minimized

Desktop & Dock	
Dock	
Size	Magnification
Small Large	Off Small Large
Position on screen	Bottom ⌄
Minimize windows using	Genie Effect ⌄
Double-click a window's title bar to	Zoom ⌄
Minimize windows into application icon	○
Automatically hide and show the Dock	○
Animate opening applications	●
Show indicators for open applications	●
Show recent applications in Dock	○

3 Drag the Dock **Size** slider to increase or decrease the size of the Dock

The **Position on screen** options enable you to place the Dock on the left, right or bottom of the screen.

4 Drag the **Magnification** slider to determine the size to which icons are enlarged when the cursor is moved over them

Move the cursor over an icon on the Dock to see the magnification effect.

5 The **Genie** effect in the **Minimize windows using** option shrinks the item to be minimized, like a genie going back into its lamp

Manual resizing

In addition to changing the size of the Dock by using the Dock settings dialog box, it can also be resized manually.

1 Drag vertically on the Dock dividing line to increase or decrease its size

Hot tip
Open windows can also be maximized and minimized by double-clicking on the Title bar (the area at the top of the window, next to the three window buttons).

Hot tip
Folders of documents can be added to the Dock. These are known as Stacks and are created by dragging a folder from a Finder window onto the right-hand side of the Dock. The files can be accessed by clicking on the Stack. Move the cursor over a Stack, then press **Ctrl** + **click** to access options for how the Stack is displayed.

Dock Menus

One of the features of the Dock is that it can display contextual menus for selected items. This means that it shows menus with options that are applicable to the item being accessed. This can only be done when an item has been opened.

1 Click and hold on the black dot below an item's icon to display the item's individual context menu

Click on **Quit** on the icon's contextual menu to close an open app or file, depending on which side of the dividing bar the item is located.

2 Click on **Show in Finder** to see where the item is located on your Mac

Working with Dock Items

Adding items

Numerous items can be added to the Dock; the only restriction is the size of monitor on which to display all of the Dock items. (The size of the Dock can be reduced to accommodate more icons, but you have to be careful that all of the icons are still legible.) To add items to the Dock:

 1 Locate the required item in the Finder and drag it onto the Dock. All the other icons move along to make space for the new one

Keep in Dock

Every time you open a new app, its icon will appear in the Dock for the duration that the app is open, even if it has not previously been put in the Dock. If you then decide that you would like to keep it in the Dock, you can enable this as follows:

1 Click and hold on the black dot below an open app's icon

2 Select **Options** > **Keep in Dock** to ensure the app remains in the Dock when it is closed

...cont'd

Removing items

Any item on the left of the dividing line, except the Finder, can be removed from the Dock. However, this does not remove it from your computer; it just removes the shortcut for accessing it. You will still be able to locate it in its folder in the Finder and, if required, drag it back onto the Dock. To remove items from the Dock:

 Drag the item away from the Dock until it displays the **Remove** tag. The item disappears once the cursor is released. All the other icons then move up to fill in the space

Removing open apps

You can remove an app from the Dock, even if it is open and running. To do this:

 Drag an app off the Dock while it is running. Initially, the icon will remain on the Dock because the app is still open

When the app is closed (click and hold on the dot below the item and select **Quit**) its icon will be removed from the Dock

Trash

The Trash folder is a location for placing items that you do not need anymore. However, when items are placed in the Trash, they are not removed from your computer. This requires another command, as the Trash is really a holding area before you decide you want to remove items permanently. The Trash can also be used for ejecting removable disks attached to your Mac.

Sending items to the Trash
Items can be sent to the Trash by dragging them from the location in which they are stored.

1 Drag an item over the **Trash** icon to place it in the Trash folder

2 Click once on the **Trash** icon on the Dock to view its contents

Items can also be sent to the Trash by selecting them in the Finder and then selecting **File** > **Move to Trash** from the Menu bar.

All items within the Trash folder can be removed in a single command: select **Finder** > **Empty Trash** from the Menu bar to remove all items in the Trash folder.

Using System Settings

In macOS there are settings that can be applied for just about every aspect of your Mac. This gives you greater control over how the interface looks and how the operating system functions. To access System Settings:

 Click on this icon on the Dock or from the Launchpad

- **Apple ID**. This contains settings for items that are to be saved to the online iCloud service (see pages 44-53).

- **Family**. This contains options for sharing a range of Apple content with up to five other family members (if it has been set up).

- **Wi-Fi**. This enables you to connect your Mac to Wi-Fi.

- **Bluetooth**. Turn this **On** to connect Bluetooth devices.

- **Network**. This contains options for connecting to available networks, for accessing the internet and other computers connected to the same network.

- **Notifications**. This determines how the Notification Center operates (see pages 36-39).

- **Sound**. This has options for setting sounds for alerts.

- **Focus**. This can be used to create conditions under which specific people and apps can or cannot contact you during certain times (see pages 40-41 for details).

- **Screen Time**. This is used to view details of your Mac use and add restrictions (see pages 162-164).

- **General**. This contains a number of options for how the Mac operates.

- **Appearance**. This contains options for the appearance of your Mac's screen, including Light and Dark mode. It also where you can specify how scroll bars operate within windows.

- **Accessibility**. This can be used for users with visual, audio or motor issues (see page 20 for details).

- **Control Center**. This determines how the Control Center operates (see pages 34-35).

- **Siri & Spotlight**. Options for turning on the digital voice assistant, and settings such as language and voice style.

- **Privacy & Security**. This can be used to activate Location Services so that your location can be used by specific apps.

- **Desktop & Dock**. This can be used to apply settings for the Desktop and also the Dock, which by default appears along the bottom of the screen.

- **Displays**. This is used to set the text size and screen brightness for the screen.

- **Wallpaper**. This is used to apply desktop backgrounds.

- **Screen Saver**. This can be used to select a graphic that is used once the screen has been inactive for a period of time.

- **Battery**. For MacBooks, this shows the battery usage of specific apps and can show the battery level in the status bar.

- **Lock Screen**. This has options for when the screen is locked after a period of inactivity, for additional security.

- **Login Password**. This is used to set, or change, a password for logging in to your Mac, or unlocking it.

- **Users & Groups**. This can be used create new user accounts so that other people can have their own account on your Mac.

- **Passwords**. This has options for managing website passwords.

- **Internet Accounts**. This can be used to link to other online accounts, such as webmail accounts.

- **Game Center**. This is used to set options for playing online games with other people.

- **Keyboard**. This contains options for how your Mac's keyboard operates.

- **Printers & Scanners**. This is used to add printers or scanners so that they can be used with your Mac.

macOS supports multiple displays, which means you can connect your Mac to two or more displays and view different content on each one. The Dock appears on the active screen, and each screen also has its own Menu bar. Different full-screen apps can also be viewed on each screen.

The **Internet Accounts** category can be used to set up email accounts with webmail services such as Google.

If a Magic Mouse or a Magic Trackpad is used with your Mac, there will be system settings for Mouse and Trackpad.

Control Center

The **Control Center** has been a feature of Apple's mobile devices – the iPhone and iPad – for a number of years, and it is also now available with macOS. It is a panel containing shortcuts to some of the most commonly-used options and functions within **System Settings**.

Accessing the Control Center

The Control Center can be accessed from the top toolbar on the Desktop or from within any app. To do this:

Focus can be used to specify times during which notifications and FaceTime calls can be muted. **Screen Mirroring** can be used to display the Mac's screen on another screen.

AirDrop is the functionality for sharing items wirelessly between compatible devices. Click once on the **AirDrop** button in the Control Center and specify whether you want to share with **Contacts Only** or **Everyone**. Once AirDrop is set up, you can use the **Share** button in compatible apps to share items such as photos with any other AirDrop users in the vicinity.

1 To open the Control Center, click on this button on the top toolbar

2 Click on these buttons to access options for **Focus**, **Stage Manager**, and **Screen Mirroring**

3 Click on these buttons to access options for turning **Wi-Fi** on or off; turning **Bluetooth** on or off; or specifying who can use **AirDrop** for sharing items

4 Click on these buttons to alter the screen brightness and the volume

5 Click on this button to access the Music widget for playing and controlling tracks from the Music app

Managing the Control Center

Items within the Control Center can be managed within System Settings.

 Open System Settings and click on the **Control Center** button

 Items in the Control Center are listed in the main window

Click on an item to view its options. If it is an item that is always in the Control Center, the only option will be to also **Show in Menu Bar**

Click on one of the Other Modules options and drag **On** the **Show in Control Center** button to add the item to the Control Center

If an item is shown in the Menu bar, it can be accessed directly from here, without having to access the Control Center.

35

Notifications and Widgets

The **Notification Center** provides a single location to view all of your emails, messages, updates and alerts. Notifications appear in the top right-hand corner of the screen. In macOS, the Notification Center now includes widgets that can display a range of useful information. Widgets can be edited within the Notification Center itself, and apps that display notifications are set up within System Settings. To do this:

Don't forget

Notifications can be accessed regardless of the app in which you are working, and they can be actioned directly without having to leave the active app.

Don't forget

Twitter and Facebook feeds can also be set up to appear in the Notification Center, if you have accounts with these sites.

Don't forget

To disable an item so that it does not appear in the Notification Center, select it as in Step 2 and drag **Off** the **Allow notifications** box in Step 3.

1 Open System Settings and click on the **Notifications** button

 Notifications

2 General notification options can be selected in the top section of the main panel. Click on an item to select it and set its notification options

3 Drag the **Allow notifications** button **On** to enable notifications for items and make selections as required for how the notifications operate

...cont'd

Viewing notifications

Notifications appear in the Notification Center. The way they appear can be determined in System Settings.

 1 Select an alert style. A banner alert comes up on the screen and then disappears after a few seconds

 2 The **Alerts** option shows the notification, and it stays on screen until dismissed (such as this one for **Reminders**)

3 Click on this clock in the top right-hand corner of the screen to view all items in the Notification Center. Click on it again to hide the Notification Center

4 Notifications that have been set up in System Settings appear at the top of the Notification Center. Widgets appear below any notifications

Hot tip

The Notification Center can also be displayed using a trackpad or Magic Trackpad by dragging with three fingers from right to left, starting from the far-right edge.

Don't forget

Software updates can also appear in the Notification Center, when they are available.

37

...cont'd

Using widgets

Widgets that appear in the Notification Center display can be managed and edited directly from the Notification Center panel. To do this:

 Swipe down to the bottom of the Notification Center in Step 4 on page 37 and tap on the **Edit Widgets** button

 Existing widgets in the Notification Center are shown in the right-hand panel. The middle panel displays widgets that can be added to the Notification Center

 All available widgets are shown in the left-hand panel. Click on one to view details about it in the middle panel so that it can be added to the Notification Center, if required

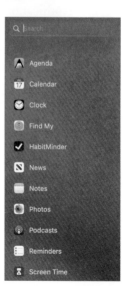

Don't forget

Click on this button in the top left-hand corner of a widget in Step 2 to remove it from the Notification Center:

4 Click on a widget in the middle panel to add it to the Notification Center, or move the cursor over the widget and tap on the green **+** button

5 Some widgets have an option for adding them to the Notification Center at different sizes. If this is available for a widget, these buttons will appear below the widget in the middle panel in Step 2 on the previous page. The options are for **Small (S)**, **Medium (M)** or **Large (L)**

Hot tip

Several versions of the same widget can be added to the Notification Center, at different sizes, if required.

Hot tip

Some widgets can be edited to display different information – for instance, the **Weather** widget can display forecasts from numerous locations around the world. To see if a widget is editable, move the cursor over it in the right-hand panel in Step 2 on the previous page. If the widget is editable, click on the **Edit Widget** button.

Reminders
Edit Widget

The Focus feature contains Do Not Disturb, which was a stand-alone feature in earlier versions of macOS. To set this up, click on the **Do Not Disturb** button in Step 2 and select the required options, and times, for when you want Do Not Disturb to operate.

Focus

Another option for managing your notifications is the **Focus** function, which can be used to control when you are notified for certain items. The Focus function can be used to limit notifications when you are performing certain actions – e.g. reading or relaxing – and it can also specify certain people and apps that are allowed to contact you and send notifications. The Focus function can be set up within System Settings, and also accessed from the Control Center. To do this:

1 Access **System Settings > Focus**

2 Click on the **Add Focus...** button

Add Focus...

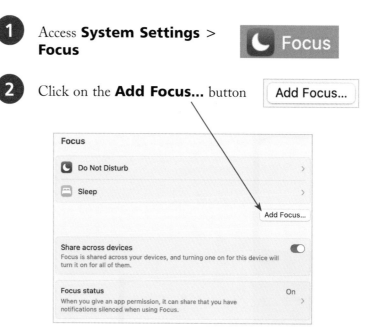

Different Focuses can be set for specific activities, and the settings for the Focus can be applied according to the required activity.

3 Click on the type of Focus that you want to add; e.g. **Personal**

4 Click on one of the **Allow Notifications**, **Allowed People**, or **Allowed Apps** options

If you add too many people in Step 5, this could negate the effect of using the specific Focus.

5 For each option in Step 4, make the relevant selections; e.g. for Allowed People, click on the **Add People** button to select people who can contact you even when the Focus is active

Once a Focus has been created, access the Control Center as shown on page 34 and click on the **Focus** button to add more Focuses, turn existing ones **On** or **Off**, and view their details.

6 Once new Focuses have been created they are displayed on the main **Focus** page within System Settings, from where they can also be edited

Drag **On** the **Share across devices** button in Step 6 to apply the Focus to all of your Apple devices sharing the same Apple ID.

7 Click on the **Add Focus...** button again in Step 2 on the previous page to create another Focus

41

Stage Manager was introduced in macOS Ventura.

Stage Manager

This is a function that can be used to minimize currently-open apps at the left-hand side of the screen, leaving the active app in the center of the screen. To activate and use **Stage Manager**:

1 Click on this button on the top toolbar to access the Control Center

2 Click the **Stage Manager** button

3 The currently-active app is displayed in the center of the screen, with the other open apps minimized as thumbnails at the left-hand side

4 Click on an app at the left-hand side to make it the active one in Stage Manager. The app can then be used in the same way as usual; i.e. surfing web pages in Safari

5 Groups of apps can also be created in Stage Manager. To do this, drag the required apps from the left-hand side into the center of the screen

6 The next time another app is made active in Stage Manager, the group of apps is minimized at the left-hand side, with their individual icons displayed

7 To specify settings for Stage Manager, access **System Settings** > **Desktop & Dock**, scroll down the page to the **Stage Manager** option and click on the **Customize...** button

Stage Manager
Stage Manager arranges your recent windows into a single strip for reduced clutter and quick access.   Customize...

8 Make selections for the operation of Stage Manager, as required, and click on the **Done** button

Recent applications
Desktop items
Show windows from an application   All at Once

Done

Don't forget

The option in Step 7 can also be used to turn the Stage Manager feature **On** or **Off**. It can also be turned **Off** by clicking on this button in the Control Center:

Stage Manager

Using iCloud

Cloud computing is an attractive proposition and one that has gained great popularity in recent years. As a concept, it consists of storing your content on an external computer server. This not only gives you added security in terms of backing up your information; it also means that the content can then be shared over a variety of devices.

iCloud is Apple's consumer cloud-computing product that consists of online services such as email; a calendar; notes; contacts; and saving photos and documents. iCloud provides users with a way to save and back up their files and content to the online service, and then use them across their Apple devices such as other Mac computers, iPhones and iPads.

About iCloud

Once iCloud has been set up (see the next page) it can be accessed from within **System Settings**.

The standard iCloud service is free, and this includes an iCloud email address and 5GB of online storage. (*Correct at the time of printing.*)

 Click on the **Apple ID** option

 Click on the **iCloud** button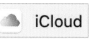

You can use iCloud to save and share the following between your different devices, with an Apple ID account (see the next page):

● Photos

● Mail and Safari

● Documents

● Backups

● Notes

● Reminders

● Contacts and Calendar

When you save an item to iCloud it automatically pushes it to all of your other compatible devices; you do not have to manually sync anything as iCloud does it all for you.

There is also a version of iCloud for Windows, which can be accessed for download from the Apple website at **https://support.apple. com/en-us/HT204283**

44

...cont'd

Setting up iCloud

To use iCloud with macOS you need to first have an Apple ID. This is a service you can register for to be able to access a range of Apple facilities, including iCloud. You can register with an email address and a password. When you first start using iCloud you will be prompted for your Apple ID details. If you do not have an Apple ID you can create one at this point.

1 Open System Settings and click on the **Sign in with your Apple ID** option

When you have an Apple ID and an iCloud account, you can also use the iCloud website to access your content. Access the website at **www.icloud.com** and log in with your Apple ID details.

2 Sign in with your Apple ID username and password, or

3 Click on the **Create Apple ID...** link and follow the steps to create your Apple ID

Create Apple ID...

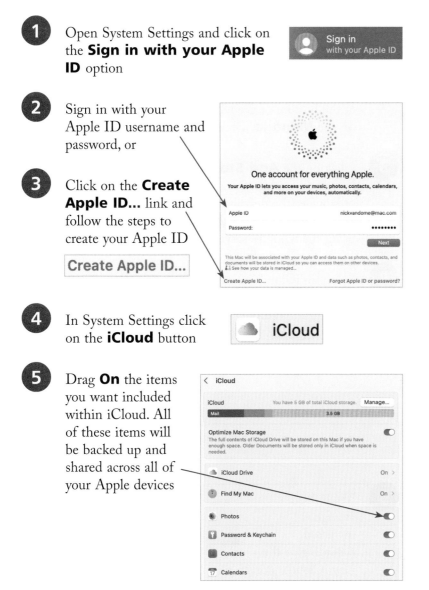

One account for everything Apple.

Your Apple ID lets you access your music, photos, contacts, calendars, and more on your devices, automatically.

Apple ID   nickvandome@mac.com

Password: ••••••••

Next

This Mac will be associated with your Apple ID and data such as photos, contacts, and documents will be stored in iCloud so you can access them on other devices. See how your data is managed...

Create Apple ID...   Forgot Apple ID or password?

The online iCloud service includes your online email service; Contacts; Calendars; Reminders; Notes; and versions of Pages, Keynote, and Numbers. You can log in to your iCloud account from any internet-enabled device.

4 In System Settings click on the **iCloud** button

 iCloud

5 Drag **On** the items you want included within iCloud. All of these items will be backed up and shared across all of your Apple devices

< iCloud

iCloud   You have 5 GB of total iCloud storage.   Manage...

Mail   3.5 GB

Optimize Mac Storage
The full contents of iCloud Drive will be stored on this Mac if you have enough space. Older Documents will be stored only in iCloud when space is needed.

☁ iCloud Drive   On >

📍 Find My Mac   On >

✿ Photos

🔑 Password & Keychain

👤 Contacts

📅 Calendars

The iCloud Drive option can be used to store items created in the Pages, Numbers, and Keynote productivity apps. Documents are stored in the Files app, and they can be stored and accessed here and from iCloud.

Upgrading to iCloud+

iCloud+ is an enhancement to iCloud that enables you to add more storage to your iCloud account and also access new security options. To subscribe to iCloud+:

 Click on the **iCloud** button as shown in Step 4 on page 45

 The amount of storage that has been used is indicated by the colored bar at the bottom of the window (e.g. blue for email). Click on the **Manage...** button

 Click on the **Add Storage** button to increase the amount of storage (the default amount is 5GB, which is provided free of charge), using the iCloud+ service

 Select an iCloud+ storage plan and click on the **Next** button to confirm the selection

5 The iCloud storage is increased, according to the new iCloud+ storage plan

6 Click on the **Options...** button next to **Private Relay** and **Hide My Email**, in the main iCloud window, to use these for internet and email security options

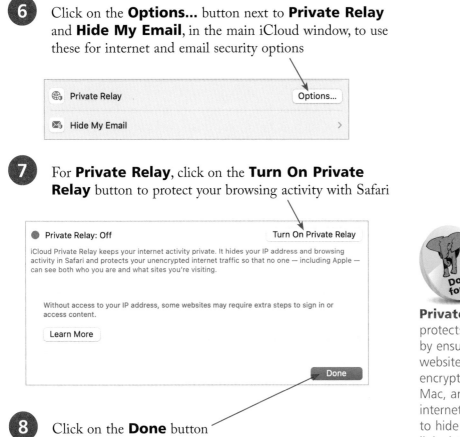

7 For **Private Relay**, click on the **Turn On Private Relay** button to protect your browsing activity with Safari

Private Relay
protects your browsing by ensuring that any website interactions are encrypted from your Mac, and two separate internet relays are used to hide the IP address linked to your Mac.

8 Click on the **Done** button

9 For **Hide My Email**, click on the **+** button to allow websites to create a random email address that is used to forward messages to your own email account so that people cannot see your email address

47

About Family Sharing

As everyone gets more and more digital devices it is becoming increasingly important to be able to share content with other people, particularly family members. In macOS, the **Family Sharing** function enables you to share items that you have downloaded from the Apple stores, such as music and movies, with up to five other family members, as long as they have an Apple ID. Once this has been set up, it is also possible to share items such as family calendars and purchases, and even subscriptions to some of Apple's online content services, such as Apple TV+. To set up and start using Family Sharing:

Hot tip

If you create a child account in Step 4 you can specify that they have to ask permission before downloading content from the iTunes Store, the App Store or the Book Store. To do this, select them in the **Family Sharing** section and drag the **Ask To Buy** button **On**. For each purchase you will be sent a notification asking for approval.

 Access the **Apple ID** section within the System Settings app, as shown on page 44

 Click on the **Family Sharing** button

 Details about Family Sharing are displayed. Click on the **Set Up Family** button to invite family members or friends to join your Family Sharing group

Family

Share your subscriptions and music, movie, and other media purchases with up to five people.

Share Subscriptions
Share current and future subscriptions, including iCloud+, Apple Music and Apple TV+.

Share Purchases
Share your apps, movies, TV shows, and books.

Set Up Parental Controls
Set up Screen Time, content restrictions and other controls for child accounts.

Set Up Family

Set Up Family

 Click on the **Invite People** button to invite another family member

Invite people to your family

Get started by inviting up to five people to join your family.

You can invite family members using Messages, Mail or AirDrop. You can also create an account for a child in your family.

Create Child Account   Not Now   Invite People

5 Select a method for sending the invitation – e.g. by email – and click on the **Continue** button

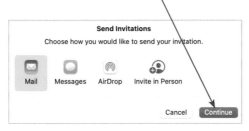

6 An invitation is created automatically (although the text can be edited), with a link in the message that is used by the recipient to activate the invitation. Send the message in the usual way for the selected option

A Family Sharing invitation has to be accepted for the recipient to join the Family Sharing group.

7 On the main Family Sharing page click on the **Subscriptions**, **Purchase Sharing** and **Location Sharing** options to view details of these items

Don't forget

The regular Apple TV option can be used to rent or buy movies and TV shows. Both the regular service and Apple TV+ can be accessed from the **TV** app.

Don't forget

The expanded iCloud service (iCloud+) can be made available via Family Sharing, giving access to additional levels of shared storage.

Don't forget

Although Apple One is not directly linked to Family Sharing, it offers similar subscription services and can be more cost-effective.

...cont'd

Using Family Sharing

Once you have set up Family Sharing and added family members, you can start sharing a selection of items.

Sharing subscriptions

There are a number of Apple subscription services, and if you join any of them then you can also share them via Family Sharing. This means that anyone in your Family Sharing group can take advantage of these services too, without having to pay for an additional subscription. The options include:

- **Apple Music**. If a family subscription has been taken out for Apple Music, this can be shared via Family Sharing, providing access to millions of songs.

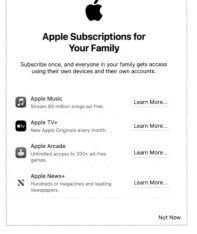

- **Apple TV+**. This is Apple's subscription service for movies and TV shows. There is a wealth of original content in Apple TV+ that you cannot access elsewhere.

- **Apple Arcade**. This is a subscription gaming service, with a range of original games that can be played individually or as multiplayer games with other people.

- **Apple News+**. This an expanded version of the free news service provided by the News app.

Apple One subscription

There is also an option for subscribing to a **Family** package that provides access to Apple Music, Apple TV+, Apple Arcade and Apple News+. This can be accessed from **System Settings** > **Apple ID** > **Media & Purchases** > **Subscriptions** > **Manage**.

Sharing calendars

Family Sharing also generates a Family calendar that can be used by all Family Sharing members.

1 Click on the **Calendar** app

2 Click on this button and create a new event (see page 107)

3 Click here and select **Family** as the calendar option to distribute the event to your Family Sharing members

Don't forget

When someone in the Family Sharing group adds an event to the Family calendar it will appear in your calendar with the appropriate tag. A red notification will also appear on the Calendar app, and it will appear in the Notification Center (if the calendar has been selected to appear here).

Sharing apps, music, books and movies

Family Sharing means that all members of the group can share purchases from the iTunes Store, the App Store or the Book Store, accessed from within the Books app. This is done from the **Purchased** section of each app.

1 Open the relevant app and access the **Purchased** section. (For the **App Store**, click on the Account icon and click on the **Purchased** button; for the **iTunes Store**, click on the **Menu** > **Purchased** button on the bottom toolbar; for the **Books** app, click on the Account icon). Click on the arrows next to someone's name to see other items that have been downloaded by other family members

Account

Purchased by Nick ⌄

2 For all three apps, click on a member under **Family Purchases** to view their purchases and download them, if required, by tapping once on this button

51

Don't forget

Family Sharing makes it easy to keep in touch with the rest of the family and see exactly where they are. This can be done with the **Find My** app. The other person must have their Apple device turned **On** and be online. To find family members, tap once on the **Find My** app. The location of any people who are linked via your Family Sharing group is displayed.

iCloud Shared Photo Library

In addition to Family Sharing, macOS also enables iCloud to create a shared photo library that can then be shared with family and friends. Older photos in the Photos app can also be added to a shared library. To use a shared photo library:

 Open the Photos app and select **Photos** > **Settings** from the Menu bar

 Click on the **Shared Library** option and click on the **Get Started...** button

 Click on the **Add Later** button to continue setting up the shared library, without adding other participants at this point

Don't forget

Once someone has joined a shared library they have full access to add photos and videos, and also edit or delete ones that are already in the shared library.

 Select one of the options for how existing photos are moved into the shared library and click on the **Next** button

For the **Choose Manually** option in the previous step, select the required photo(s) and click on the **Add** button

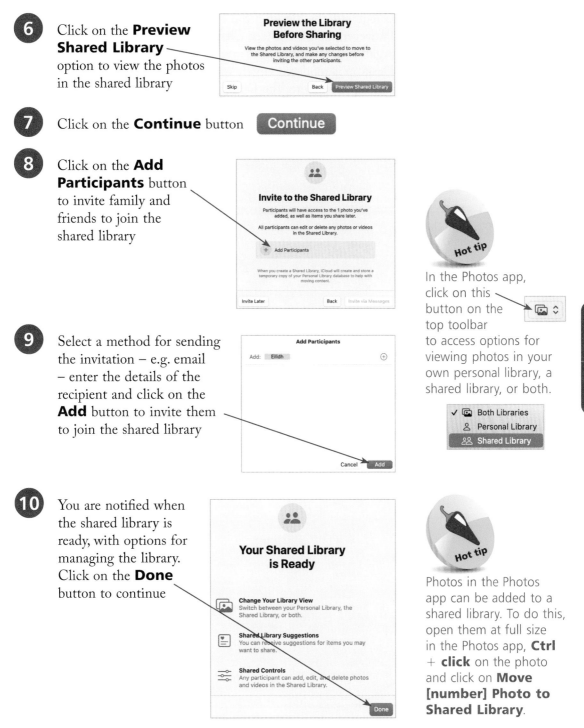

6 Click on the **Preview Shared Library** option to view the photos in the shared library

Preview the Library Before Sharing

View the photos and videos you've selected to move to the Shared Library, and make any changes before inviting the other participants.

Skip   Back   Preview Shared Library

7 Click on the **Continue** button

Continue

8 Click on the **Add Participants** button to invite family and friends to join the shared library

Invite to the Shared Library

Participants will have access to the 1 photo you've added, as well as items you share later.

All participants can edit or delete any photos or videos in the Shared Library.

+ Add Participants

When you create a Shared Library, iCloud will create and store a temporary copy of your Personal Library database to help with moving content.

Invite Later   Back   Invite via Messages

Hot tip

In the Photos app, click on this button on the top toolbar to access options for viewing photos in your own personal library, a shared library, or both.

✓ 🖼 Both Libraries
  👤 Personal Library
  👥 Shared Library

9 Select a method for sending the invitation – e.g. email – enter the details of the recipient and click on the **Add** button to invite them to join the shared library

Add Participants

Add: Eilidh   ⊕

Cancel   Add

10 You are notified when the shared library is ready, with options for managing the library. Click on the **Done** button to continue

Your Shared Library is Ready

🖼 **Change Your Library View**
Switch between your Personal Library, the Shared Library, or both.

❤ **Shared Library Suggestions**
You can receive suggestions for items you may want to share.

⚙ **Shared Controls**
Any participant can add, edit, and delete photos and videos in the Shared Library.

Done

Hot tip

Photos in the Photos app can be added to a shared library. To do this, open them at full size in the Photos app, **Ctrl + click** on the photo and click on **Move [number] Photo to Shared Library**.

Desktop Items

If required, the Desktop can be used to store apps and files. However, the Finder (see Chapter 3) does such a good job of organizing all of the elements within your computer that the Desktop is rendered largely redundant, unless you feel happier storing items here. The Desktop can also display any removable disks that are connected to your computer:

Hot tip

Icons for removable disks (e.g. flashdrives) will only become visible on the Desktop once a disk has been inserted.

If a removable disk is connected to your computer, double-click the Desktop icon to view its contents.

Don't forget

Any removable disks that are connected to your computer can also be viewed by clicking on them in the sidebar in the Finder.

Ejecting Items

If you have removable disks attached to your Mac, it is essential to be able to eject them quickly and easily. In macOS there are two ways in which this can be done:

1 In the Finder, click on this icon to the right of the name of the removable disk, or

Locations
- Nick's MacBook Pro
- FLASHDRIVE

2 On the Desktop, click and drag the disk icon over the **Trash**. This turns the Trash icon into the **Eject** icon, and the disk will be ejected

Hot tip

If the Desktop items are not showing, open the Finder and click on **Finder** > **Settings** on the Menu bar and click on the **General** tab. Under **Show these items on the desktop** drag **On** the items you want, including **Hard Disks**, **External Disks** and **CDs, DVDs, and iPods**.

3 Some disks, such as CDs and DVDs (if they are connected with an external SuperDrive), are physically ejected when either of the above two actions is performed. Other disks, such as flashdrives, have to be removed manually once they have been ejected by macOS. If the disk is not ejected first, the following warning message will appear:

Disk Not Ejected Properly
Eject "FLASHDRIVE" before disconnecting or turning it off.

Resuming

One of the chores about computing is that when you shut down your computer, you have to first close all of your open documents and apps and then open them all again when you turn your machine back on. However, macOS has a resuming feature that allows you to continue working exactly where you left off, even if you turn off your computer. To use this:

1 Before you shut down, all of your open documents and apps are available (as shown)

Beware

If you have open, unsaved documents you will be prompted to save them before your Mac is shut down.

2 Select the **Shut Down...** or **Restart...** option from the **Apple menu**

3 Make sure this box is checked **On** (this will ensure that all of your items will appear as before, after the Mac is shut down and then started up again)

 Reopen windows when logging back in

4 Confirm the **Shut Down** or **Restart** command

Are you sure you want to shut down your computer now?

If you do nothing, the computer will shut down automatically in 40 seconds.

☑ Reopen windows when logging back in

Cancel   Shut Down

3 Finder

The principal method for moving around macOS is the Finder. This enables you to access items and organize your apps, folders and files. This chapter looks at how to use the Finder and how to get the most out of this powerful tool for navigating around macOS. It covers accessing items, how to customize the interface, and options for working with folders.

Working with the Finder

If you were only able to use one item on the Dock, it would be the Finder. This is the gateway to all of the elements of your Mac. While it is possible to get to selected items through other routes, the Finder is the only location where you can gain access to everything on your system. If you ever feel that you are getting lost within macOS, click on the Finder and then you should begin to feel more at home. To access the Finder:

Don't forget

A link to iCloud Drive is also included in the Finder sidebar.

Don't forget

The **Actions** button has options for displaying information about a selected item and also options for how it is displayed within the Finder (see page 74 for details).

 1   Click once on this icon at the left-hand side of the Dock

Overview

The Finder has its own toolbar; a sidebar from which items can be accessed; and a main window, where the contents of selected items can be viewed:

View options   Actions button   Search

Recent files

Folders are displayed here in the sidebar

Tags

Main window

Hot tip

Tags in the Finder can be used to identify similar files and documents. To add tags, select the required items (see page 69) and drag a tag over them. To give tags specific names, **Ctrl + click** on one in the Finder sidebar, and click on the **Rename** option.

Finder Folders

Recents

This contains all of the latest files in which you have been working. They are sorted into categories according to file type so that you can search through them quickly. This is an excellent way to locate items without having to look through a lot of folders. To access this:

 Click on this button in the Finder sidebar to access the contents of your **Recents** folder

 All of your files are displayed in individual categories. Click on the headings at the top of each category to sort items by those criteria (in List view; see pages 61-64 for more details about Finder views)

 Double-click on an item to open it from the Finder

The Finder is always open (as denoted by the black dot below its icon on the Dock) and it cannot readily be closed down or removed.

The Finder sidebar has the macOS transparency feature so that you can see some of the open window, or Desktop, behind it.

To change the display of folders in the sidebar, click on the **Finder** menu on the top toolbar. Select **Settings** and click on the **Sidebar** tab. Under **Show these items in the sidebar:** select the items you want included.

...cont'd

Home folder

This contains the contents of your own Home directory, containing your personal folders and files. macOS inserts some pre-named folders that it thinks will be useful, but it is possible to rearrange or delete these as you please. It is also possible to add as many more folders as you want.

Don't forget

This folder contains all of the applications on your Mac. They can also be accessed from the Launchpad, as shown on pages 92-93.

📄 Documents

This is part of your Home folder but is also on the Finder sidebar for ease of access. New folders can be created for different types of documents.

① Click on your Apple ID account name in the sidebar to access the contents of your **Home** folder

🏠 **nickvandome**

② The **Home** folder contains the **Public** folder, which can be used to share files with other users if the computer is part of a network

Hot tip

When you are creating documents, macOS by default recognizes their type and then, when you save them, suggests the most applicable folder in which to save them.

③ To add a new folder, click the **Actions** button (see page 74), then **New Folder** (or **Ctrl + click** in the window and select **New Folder**). The new folder will open in the main window, named "untitled folder". Overtype the name with one of your choice

④ To delete a folder from the Finder sidebar, **Ctrl + click** on it and select **Remove from Sidebar**

Finder Views

The way in which items are displayed within the Finder can be amended in a variety of ways, depending on how you want to view the contents of a folder. Different folders can have their own viewing options applied to them, and these will stay in place until a new option is specified.

Back button

When working within the Finder, each new window replaces the previous one, unless you open a new app. This prevents the screen from becoming cluttered with dozens of open windows as you look through various Finder windows for a particular item. To ensure that you never feel lost within the Finder structure, there is a Back button on the Finder toolbar that enables you to retrace the steps that you have taken.

Hot tip

Select an item within the Finder window and tap on the space bar to view its details.

 Navigate to a folder within the Finder (in this example, the **macOS Ventura** folder contained within **Pictures**)

② Click on the **Back** button to move back to the previously-visited window (in this example, the main **Pictures** window)

Beware

If you have not opened any Finder windows, the **Back** button will not operate.

...cont'd

View options

It is possible to customize some of the options for how items are viewed in the Finder. To do this:

1 Click on this button on the Finder toolbar

2 Select **Show View Options** to access options for customizing the Finder view

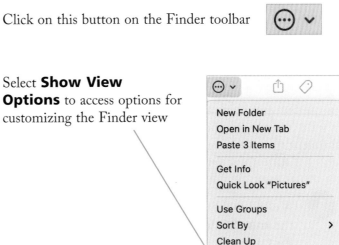

New Folder
Open in New Tab
Paste 3 Items

Get Info
Quick Look "Pictures"

Use Groups
Sort By   >
Clean Up
Clean Up By   >
Show View Options

Hot tip

A very large icon size can be useful for people with poor eyesight, but it takes up a lot more space in a window.

3 Drag this slider to set the icon size

Pictures

☑ Always open in icon view
☑ Browse in icon view

Group By: None
Sort By: None

Icon size: 84×84

Grid spacing:

Text size: 12
Label position:
● Bottom ○ Right

☐ Show item info
☑ Show icon preview

4 Select options here for the way items are arranged and displayed in Finder windows

Icon, List and Columns views

There are several options for displaying folders and files within the Finder. To access them:

1 Click on this button on the Finder toolbar

2 Select one of the view options, from **as Icons**, **as List**, **as Columns** and **as Gallery** (see page 64 for Gallery view)

✓ as Icons
as List
as Columns
as Gallery

The button in Step 1 changes in appearance, depending on the selection in Step 2.

Icon view

List view

Columns view

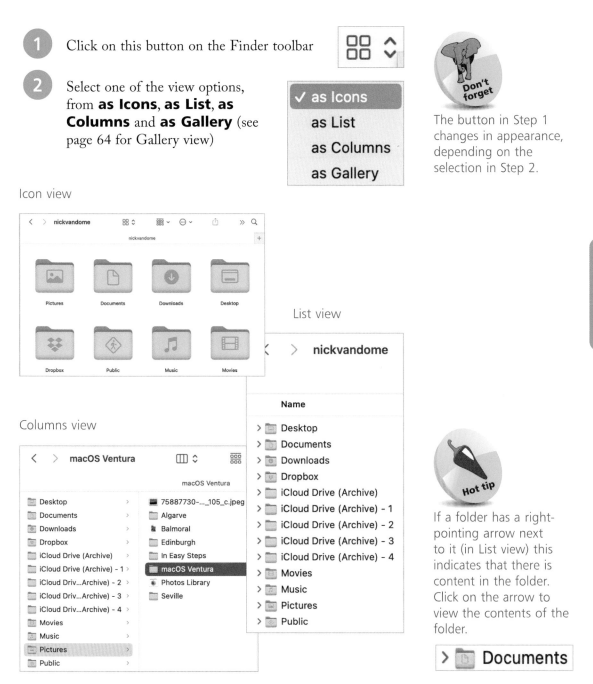

Don't forget

Hot tip

If a folder has a right-pointing arrow next to it (in List view) this indicates that there is content in the folder. Click on the arrow to view the contents of the folder.

> 📁 **Documents**

63

Gallery View

Another of the view options on the Finder toolbar is Gallery view: this is a view that has considerable functionality in terms of viewing details of specific files and also applying some quick editing functions to them without having to open the files. To use Gallery view:

 Select a file in either Icon, List or Columns view and click on the **as Gallery** option from the button on the top of the toolbar, as shown on page 63

✓ as Icons
as List
as Columns
as Gallery

as shown on page 63

2 The item is displayed in the main window, with thumbnails of the other available files below it

Hot tip

Gallery view is a good option for looking through photos without having to open the Photos app. Move through the photos by clicking on the thumbnails at the bottom of the screen, or with the arrow keys on the keyboard.

3 The item that is displayed will change depending on the type of file that is selected

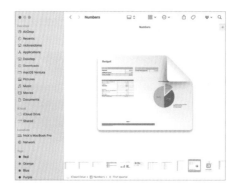

Quick Look

Through a Finder option called Quick Look, it is possible to view the content of a file without having to first open it. To do this:

1 Select a file in any of the Finder views

75887730-DAFA-4...5_c.jpeg

2 Press the space bar on the keyboard

3 The contents of the file are displayed without it opening in its default program. Click on the **Markup** button on the top toolbar to add Markup items, such as drawing or writing

65

4 Click on the cross to close Quick Look, or view the item in full screen by clicking this button

The **Markup** button provides a range of options for drawing or writing on an item, including types of pens, shapes, borders, colors and text styles.

In Quick Look it is even possible to preview videos or presentations without having to first open them in their default app. If videos are being viewed, there will be a **Trim** button so that the length of the video can be trimmed without having to open it in a specific app.

Finder Toolbar

Customizing the toolbar

As with most elements of macOS, it is possible to customize the Finder toolbar. To do this:

View	Go	Window	Help
as Icons			⌘ 1
✓ as List			⌘ 2
as Columns			⌘ 3
as Gallery			⌘ 4
✓ Use Groups			^⌘ 0
Group By			>
Clean Up			
Clean Up By			>
Hide Sidebar			^⌘ S
Show Preview			⇧⌘ P
Hide Toolbar			⌥⌘ T
Show All Tabs			⇧⌘ \
Hide Tab Bar			⇧⌘ T
Hide Path Bar			⌥⌘ P
Show Status Bar			⌘ /
Customize Toolbar...			

1 Select **View** > **Customize Toolbar...** from the Menu bar

Beware

Do not put too many items on the Finder toolbar as you may not be able to see them all in the Finder window. If there are additional toolbar items, there will be a directional arrow indicating this. Click on the arrow to view the available items.

2 Drag individual items from the window into the toolbar

Drag your favorite items into the toolbar...

< > Back/Forward	☰ ⌄ Path	🔲 Group	88 ≣ ▥ ⬜ View	⊙ Action
⏏ Eject	☢ Burn	⬜ Space	↔ Flexible Space	📁 New Folder
🗑 Delete	🖥 Connect	ⓘ Get Info	🔍 Search Search	👁 Quick Look
⬆ Share	⊘ Edit Tags	⬚ Preview	⦿ AirDrop	☁ iCloud

3 Alternatively, drag the default set of icons into the toolbar

... or drag the default set into the toolbar.

< > Back/Forward	88 ≣ ▥ ⬜ View	⬜ Space	88 ⌄ Group	⬆ Share	⊘ Edit Tags	⊙ ⌄ Action	🔍 Search Search

Show Icon Only ⊙   **Done**

4 Click **Done** at the bottom of the window   **Done**

Finder Sidebar

Using the sidebar

The sidebar is the left-hand panel of the Finder that can be used to access items on your Mac. To use this:

1 Click on a button on the sidebar

2 Its contents are displayed in the main Finder window

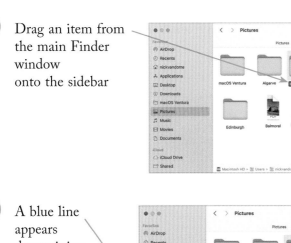

Adding to the sidebar

Items that you access most frequently can be added to the sidebar.

1 Drag an item from the main Finder window onto the sidebar

2 A blue line appears determining the location, and the item is added to the sidebar at this point. You can do this with apps, folders and files

When you click on an item in the sidebar, its contents are shown in the main Finder window to the right.

When items are added to the Finder sidebar, a shortcut – or alias – is inserted into the sidebar, not the actual item.

Items can be removed from the sidebar by **Ctrl** + **clicking** on them and selecting **Remove from Sidebar** from the contextual menu.

Working with Folders

Folders are always denoted by a folder icon. In Icon view they are larger than in List or Columns views.

You can create as many "nested" folders (i.e. folders within other folders) as you want, although this can make your folder structure more complicated. Folders can also be dragged over other folders, and if you pause before you release the first folder you will be able to view the content of the target folder, to make sure this is where you want to place the first folder. This is known as spring-loaded folders.

Content can be added to an empty folder by dragging it from another folder and dropping it into the new one.

When macOS is installed, there are various folders that have already been created to hold apps and files. Some of these are essential (i.e. those containing apps), while others are created as an aid for where you might want to store the files that you create (such as the Pictures and Movies folders). Once you start working with macOS, you will probably want to create your own folders in which to store and organize your documents. This can be done on the Desktop or within any level of your existing folder structure. To create a new folder:

1 Access the location in which you want to create a new folder (e.g. your Home folder) and select **File > New Folder** from the Menu bar

2 A new, empty folder is inserted at the selected location (named "untitled folder")

3 Overtype the file name with a new one. Press **Enter**

4 Double-click on the folder to view its contents (at this point it should be empty)

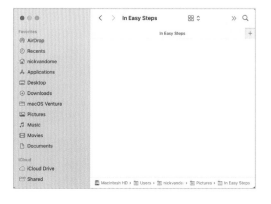

Selecting Items

Apps and files within macOS folders can be selected by a variety of different methods.

Selecting by dragging

Click and drag the cursor to encompass the items to be selected. The selected items will become highlighted.

Once items have been selected, a single command can be applied to all of them. For instance, you can copy a group of items by selecting them and then applying the **Copy** command from the Menu bar.

Selecting by clicking

Click once on an item to select it, hold down **Shift**, and then click on another item in the list to select a consecutive group of items.

To select all of the items in a folder, select **Edit** > **Select All** from the Menu bar. The **Select All** command selects all of the elements within the active item. For instance, if the active item is a word processing document, the **Select All** command will select all of the items within the document; if it is a folder, it will select all of the items within that folder. You can also click **Command** + **A** to select all items.

To select a non-consecutive group, select the first item by clicking on it once, then hold down the Command key (**cmd ⌘**) and select the other required items. The selected items will appear highlighted.

Copying and Moving Items

Items can be copied and moved within macOS by using the copy and paste method, or by dragging.

Copy and paste

Don't forget

When an item is copied, it is placed on the Clipboard and remains there until another item is copied.

1 Select an item (or items) and select **Edit** > **Copy** from the Menu bar

Edit	View	Go	Windov
Undo			⌘ Z
Redo			⇧ ⌘ Z
Cut			⌘ X
Copy 5 Items			⌘ C
Paste			⌘ V
Select All			⌘ A

2 Move to the target location and select **Edit** > **Paste Item(s)** from the Menu bar. The item is then pasted into the new location

Edit	View	Go	Windov
Undo			⌘ Z
Redo			⇧ ⌘ Z
Cut		●	⌘ X
Copy			⌘ C
Paste 5 Items			⌘ V
Select All			⌘ A

Hot tip

Since 2016, macOS has supported the Universal Clipboard, where items can be copied on a device such as an iPhone and then pasted directly into a document on a Mac running macOS. The mobile device has to be running iOS 10 (or later) and the Mac has to support the Universal Clipboard. The process is the same as regular copy and paste, except that each operation is performed on each separate device and each app used has to be set up for iCloud. Also, Bluetooth and Wi-Fi have to be activated on both devices.

3 To view items that have been copied onto the clipboard, select **Edit** > **Show Clipboard** from the Menu bar. The items are displayed in the Clipboard window

Edit	View	Go	Windov
Undo			⌘ Z
Redo			⇧ ⌘ Z
Cut			⌘ X
Copy			⌘ C
Paste 5 Items			⌘ V
Select All			⌘ A
Show Clipboard			

```
● ● ●                    Clipboard
Screenshot 2022-11-24 at 11.06.35 AM
Screenshot 2022-11-24 at 11.06.01 AM
Screenshot 2022-11-24 at 11.05.33 AM
Screenshot 2022-11-24 at 11.05.22 AM
Screenshot 2022-11-24 at 11.05.09 AM
```

Dragging

Drag a file from one location to another to move it to that location. (This requires two or more Finder windows to be open, or drag the item over a folder on the sidebar.)

Finder Search

Searching electronic data is now a massive industry, with companies such as Google leading the way with online searching. On Macs it is also possible to search your folders and files, using the built-in search facilities: Finder search (see page 16); Siri (see pages 17-19); or Spotlight search (see pages 15-16).

Using Finder

To search for items within the Finder:

Try to make your search keywords and phrases as accurate as possible. This will create a better list of search results.

1 In the Finder window, click on this icon on the top toolbar and enter the search keyword(s) in the box. Search options are listed below the keyword

2 Select an option for which category you want to search over

3 The search results are shown in the Finder window. Click on one of these buttons to search specific areas

Both folders and files will be displayed in the Finder as part of the search results.

4 Double-click on an item to open it

Finder Tabs

Tabs in web browsers are now well established and allow you to have several pages open within the same browser window. This technology is included in the Finder in macOS, with Finder tabs. This enables different folders to be open in different tabs within the Finder so that you can organize your content exactly how you want. To do this:

In macOS, tabs are available in a range of apps that open multiple windows, including the Apple productivity apps: Pages, Numbers, and Keynote. If the tabs are not showing, select **View** > **Show Tab Bar** from the app's Menu bar.

1 Select **View** > **Show Tab Bar** from the Finder menu

View	Go	Window	Help
✓ as Icons			⌘1
as List			⌘2
as Columns			⌘3
as Gallery			⌘4
Use Groups			⌃⌘0
Sort By			>
Clean Up			
Clean Up By			>
Hide Sidebar			⌃⌘S
Show Preview			⇧⌘P
Hide Toolbar			⌥⌘T
Show All Tabs			⇧⌘\
Show Tab Bar			⇧⌘T

2 A new tab appears at the right-hand side of the Finder

3 Click on this button to open the new tab

4 At this point, the content in the new tab is displayed in the window (see the second Hot tip)

To specify an option for what appears in the default window for a new Finder window tab, click on the **Finder** menu and click on **Settings**, then the **General** tab. Under **New Finder windows show:**, select the default window to be used.

5 Access a new folder to display this as the content for the tab. In this way, you can use different tabs for different types of content such as Recents, or photos, or for topics such as Work, Travel or Finance within Documents

Beware

Dozens of tabs can be added in the Finder. However, when there are too many to fit along the Tab bar they are stacked on top of each other, so it can be hard to work out what you have in your tabs.

6 Each tab view can be customized, and this is independent of the other tabs

Actions Button

The Finder **Actions** button provides a variety of options for any item or items selected in the Finder. To use this:

Icons on the Finder toolbar can be changed by customizing them – see page 66.

1 Select an item or group of items about which you want to find out additional information

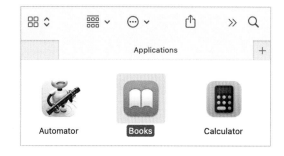

The **Actions** button can also be used for labeling items with Finder tags. To do this, select the required items in the Finder and click one of the colored dots at the bottom of the **Actions** button menu. The selected tag will be applied to the item names in the Finder. Tagged items can be searched for by clicking on the required tag in the sidebar. Matching items will be shown in the main Finder window.

2 Click on the **Actions** button on the Finder toolbar

3 The available options for the selected item or items are displayed. These include **Get Info**, which displays additional information about an item such as file type, file size, creation and modification dates, and the default app for opening the item(s)

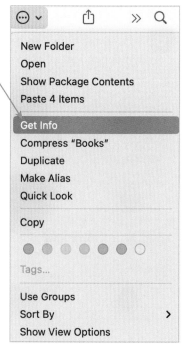

Sharing from the Finder

Also on the Finder toolbar is the Share button. This can be used to share a selected item or items in a variety of ways appropriate to the type of file that has been selected. For instance, a photo will have options including social media sites such as Twitter, while a text document will have fewer options. To share items directly from the Finder:

1 Locate and select item(s) that you want to share

This button on the Finder is for changing the arrangement of items within the Finder. Click on this to access arrangement options such as Name, Date and Size:

2 Click on the **Share** button on the Finder toolbar

3 Select one of the options for sharing the item selected in Step 1

Menus

The main Apple Menu bar in macOS contains a variety of menus that are accessed when the Finder is the active window. When individual apps are open they have their own Menu bars, although in a lot of cases these are similar to the standard Menu bar, particularly for the built-in macOS apps such as Calendar, Contacts and Notes.

- **Apple menu**. This is denoted by an apple icon and contains general information about the computer, links to System Settings and the App Store for app updates, and options for shutting down your Mac.

- **Finder menu**. This contains settings for amending the functionality and appearance of the Finder, and also options for emptying the Trash and accessing other apps (under the Services option).

- **File menu**. This contains common commands for working with open documents, such as opening and closing files, creating aliases, moving files or documents to the Trash, ejecting external devices, and burning discs.

- **Edit menu**. This contains common commands that apply to the majority of apps used on the Mac. These include Undo, Cut, Copy, Paste, Select All, and Show the contents of the Clipboard; i.e. items that have been cut or copied.

- **View menu**. This contains options for how windows and folders are displayed within the Finder, and for customizing the Finder toolbar. This includes showing or hiding the Finder sidebar and selecting view options for the size at which icons are displayed within Finder windows.

- **Go menu**. This can be used to navigate around your computer. This includes moving files or documents to your Recents folder, your Home folder, your Applications folder and recently-accessed folders.

- **Window menu**. This contains commands to organize currently-open apps and files on your Desktop.

- **Help menu**. This contains Mac Help files, which contain information about all aspects of macOS.

4 Navigating in macOS

*macOS has Multi-Touch
Gestures for navigating
around your apps and
documents. This chapter looks
at how to use these to get
around your Mac and also at
using Mission Control.*

The macOS Way of Navigating

One of the most revolutionary features of macOS was the way in which you can navigate around your applications, web pages and documents. This involves a much greater reliance on swiping on a trackpad or adapted mouse; techniques that have been imported from the iPhone and the iPad. These are known as Multi-Touch Gestures, and to take full advantage of these you will need to have one of the following devices:

- **A trackpad**. This can be found on MacBooks.

- **A Magic Trackpad**. This can be used with an iMac, a Mac mini or a Mac Pro. It works wirelessly via Bluetooth.

- **A Magic Mouse**. This can be used with an iMac, a Mac mini or a Mac Pro. It works wirelessly via Bluetooth.

All of these devices work using a swiping technique with fingers moving over their surface. This should be done with a light touch; it is a gentle swipe, rather than any pressure being applied to the device.

The trackpads and Magic Mouse do not have any buttons in the same way as traditional devices. Instead, specific areas are clickable so that you can still perform left- and right-click operations.

On a Magic Mouse, the center and right side can be used for clicking operations, and on a Magic Trackpad, the left and right corners can perform the same tasks.

Hot tip

Models of MacBooks from May 2015 onward (and the Magic Trackpad) employ a technology known as Force Touch. This provides the user with different options, depending on how firmly they press on the trackpad. This means that more than one function can be performed, simply by pressing more firmly on the trackpad. It also provides haptic feedback, which is a physical response from the trackpad in the form of a small vibration, once different options have been accessed.

macOS Scroll Bars

In macOS, scroll bars in web pages and documents are reactive to the navigational device being used on the computer. By default, with a Magic Trackpad, a trackpad or a Magic Mouse, scroll bars are only visible when scrolling is actually taking place. However, if a mouse is being used they will be visible permanently, although this can be changed for all devices. To perform scrolling with macOS:

If you do not have a trackpad, a Magic Trackpad or a Magic Mouse, you can still navigate in macOS with a traditional mouse and the use of scroll bars in windows.

1 Scroll around a web page or document by swiping up or down on a Magic Mouse, a Magic Trackpad, or a trackpad. As you move up or down, a scroll bar appears

For instructions on scrolling with a Magic Mouse, see page 86. For scrolling with a Magic Trackpad, see page 83.

2 When you stop scrolling, the bar disappears to allow an optimum viewing area for your web page or document

3 To change the scroll bar options, select **System Settings** > **Appearance** and select the required settings under **Show scroll bars**

Show scroll bars
- ● Automatically based on mouse or trackpad
- ○ When scrolling
- ○ Always

Split View

When working with computers it can sometimes be beneficial to be able to view two windows next to each other. This can be to compare information in two different windows, or just to be able to use two windows without having to access them from the Desktop each time. In macOS, two windows can be displayed next to each other using the **Split View** feature.

 By default, all open windows are layered on top of each other, with the active one at the top

Don't forget

If you click once on the green maximize button this will display the app in full-screen mode, rather than holding on it to activate **Split View**.

80

Press and hold on the green maximize button and select either **Tile Window to Left of Screen** or **Tile Window to Right of Screen** to position the window accordingly

Click on one of the apps on the right-hand side in Step 2 on the previous page to add it as the other **Split View** panel. Click on each window to make it active

You can work in one panel in **Split View** (i.e. move through web pages) without affecting the content of the app on the other side.

 Drag the middle divider bar to resize either of the **Split View** panels, to change the viewing area

Swap the windows in **Split View** by dragging the top toolbar of one app into the other window.

 Move the cursor over the top of the window of each **Split View** item to view its toolbar and controls

Trackpad Gestures

Pointing and clicking

A Magic Trackpad, or trackpad, can be used to perform a variety of pointing and clicking tasks.

82

 Tap with one finger in the middle of the Magic Trackpad or trackpad to perform a single-click operation; e.g. to click on a button or click on an open window

2 Tap once with two fingers in the middle of the Magic Trackpad or trackpad to access any contextual menus associated with an item (this is the equivalent of the traditional right-click with a mouse)

3 Press and hold with one finger to access data detectors for selected items. This is a content-specific function depending on the selected item: if it is a web page link it will show it in a pop-up window; if it is a calendar-related word – e.g. "tomorrow" – it will create a new calendar event

 Swipe left with three fingers from the right-hand edge of the Magic Trackpad or trackpad to access the Notification Center

Scrolling and zooming

One of the most common operations on a computer is scrolling on a page, whether it is a web page or a document. Traditionally, this has been done with a mouse and a cursor. However, using a Magic Trackpad you can now do all of your scrolling with your fingers. There are a number of options for doing this.

Scrolling up and down

To move up and down web pages or documents, use two fingers on the Magic Trackpad or trackpad, and swipe up or down. The page moves in the opposite direction to the one in which you are swiping – i.e. if you swipe up, the page moves down, and vice versa.

Beware

If you have too many functions set using the same number of fingers, some of them may not work. See pages 87-88 for details about applying settings for Multi-Touch Gestures.

 Open a web page

 Position two fingers in the middle of the Magic Trackpad or trackpad

3 Swipe them up to move down the page

Don't forget

When scrolling up and down pages, the gesture moves the page the opposite way – i.e. swipe down to move up the page, and vice versa.

 Swipe them down to move up the page

...cont'd

Zooming in and out

To zoom in or out on web pages or documents:

Pages can also be zoomed in on by double-tapping with two fingers.

1 To zoom in, position your thumb and forefinger in the middle of the Magic Trackpad or trackpad

2 Spread them outward to zoom in on a web page or document

There is a limit on how far you can zoom in or out on a web page or document, to ensure that it does not distort the content too much.

3 To zoom out, position your thumb and forefinger at opposite corners of the Magic Trackpad or trackpad

4 Pinch them into the center of the Magic Trackpad or trackpad, to zoom out

Moving between pages

With Multi-Touch Gestures, it is possible to swipe between pages within a document (such as a book). To do this:

 Position two fingers to the left or right of the Magic Trackpad or trackpad

 Swipe to the opposite side of the Magic Trackpad or trackpad, to move through the document

Moving between full-screen apps

In addition to moving between pages by swiping, it is also possible to move between different apps when they are in full-screen mode. To do this:

 Position three fingers to the left or right of the Magic Trackpad or trackpad

 Swipe to the opposite side of the Magic Trackpad or trackpad, to move through the available full-screen apps

Showing the Desktop

To show the whole Desktop, regardless of how many files or apps are open:

 Position your thumb and three fingers in the middle of the Magic Trackpad or trackpad

Swipe to the opposite corners of the Magic Trackpad or trackpad, to display the Desktop

The Desktop is displayed, with all items minimized around the side of the screen

See pages 94-95 for details about using full-screen apps.

Magic Mouse Gestures

Pointing and clicking
A Magic Mouse can be used to perform a variety of pointing and clicking tasks.

 Click with one finger on the Magic Mouse to perform a single-click operation; e.g. to select a button or command

 Tap with one finger on the right side of the Magic Mouse to access any contextual menus associated with an item (this is the equivalent of the traditional right-click with a mouse)

Scrolling and zooming
The Magic Mouse can also be used to perform scrolling and zooming functions within a web page or document.

 Swipe up or down with one finger to move up or down a web page or document. Double-tap with one finger to zoom in on a web page

 Swipe left or right with one finger to move between pages

 Swipe left or right with two fingers to move between full-screen apps

Don't forget

When scrolling on a web page or document, it moves in the opposite direction to the movement of your finger – i.e. if you swipe up, the page moves down, and vice versa.

Multi-Touch Settings

Some Multi-Touch Gestures only have a single action, which cannot be changed. However, others have options for changing the action linked to a specific gesture. This is done within the respective settings for the Magic Mouse, the Magic Trackpad or the trackpad, where a full list of Multi-Touch Gestures is shown. To use these:

1 Access **System Settings** and click on the **Mouse** or **Trackpad** button

2 Click on one of the tabs at the top

3 The actions are described on the left, with a graphic explanation on the right

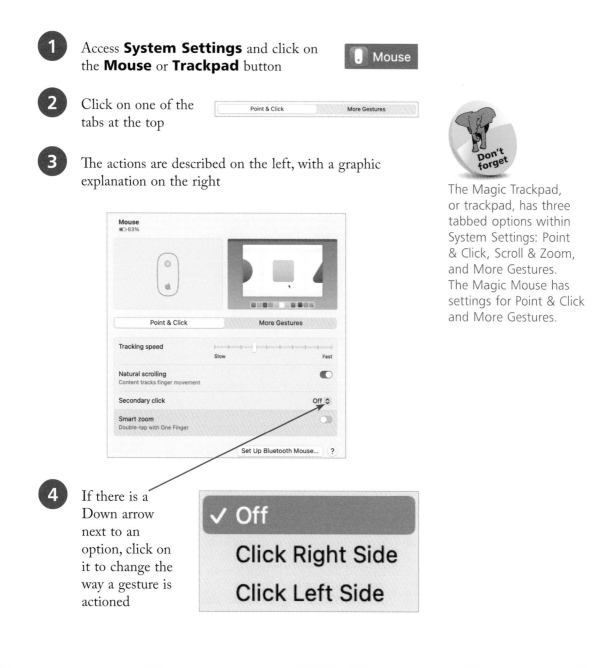

4 If there is a Down arrow next to an option, click on it to change the way a gesture is actioned

The Magic Trackpad, or trackpad, has three tabbed options within System Settings: Point & Click, Scroll & Zoom, and More Gestures. The Magic Mouse has settings for Point & Click and More Gestures.

Don't forget

...cont'd

Trackpad gestures

The full list of trackpad Multi-Touch Gestures, with their default actions, is (relevant ones for the Magic Mouse are in brackets):

Point & Click

- Tap to click – tap once with one finger (same for the Magic Mouse).

- Secondary click – click or tap with two fingers (single-click on the right of the Magic Mouse).

- Lookup and data detectors – press and hold with one finger.

Scroll & Zoom

- Scroll direction: natural – with two fingers, content tracks finger movement (one finger with the Magic Mouse).

- Zoom in or out – spread or pinch with two fingers.

- Smart zoom – double-tap with two fingers (double-tap with one finger with the Magic Mouse).

- Rotate – rotate with two fingers.

More gestures

- Swipe between pages – scroll left or right with two fingers (scroll left or right with one finger with the Magic Mouse).

- Swipe between full-screen apps – swipe left or right with three fingers (swipe left or right with two fingers with the Magic Mouse).

- Swipe left with three fingers from the right-hand edge of the trackpad or Magic Trackpad to access the Notification Center.

- Access Mission Control (see the next page) – swipe up with three fingers (double-tap with two fingers with the Magic Mouse).

- App Exposé – swipe down with three fingers.

- Access Launchpad – pinch with thumb and three fingers.

- Show Desktop – spread with thumb and three fingers.

Don't forget

Natural scrolling means the page follows the direction of your finger, vertically or horizontally, depending on which way you're scrolling.

Hot tip

Exposé enables you to view all active windows that are currently open for a particular app.

Mission Control

Mission Control is a function in macOS that helps you organize all of your open apps, full-screen apps, and documents. It also enables you to quickly view the Desktop. Within Mission Control there are also Spaces, where you can group similar types of documents together. To use Mission Control:

Don't forget

Click on a window in Mission Control to access it and exit the Mission Control window.

1 Click on this button in the Launchpad, or swipe upward with three fingers on the Magic Trackpad or trackpad, or double-tap with two fingers on a Magic Mouse

Mission Control

2 All open files and apps are visible via Mission Control

Beware

Any apps or files that have been minimized or closed do not appear within the main Mission Control window. Instead, they are located to the right of the dividing line on the Dock.

3 If there is more than one window open for an app they will each be shown separately

4 Move the cursor over the top of the Mission Control window to view the different Spaces (see page 90) and any apps in full-screen mode

Desktop 1   Desktop 2

Hot tip

Drag an open app to the top of the screen to access Mission Control. You can then make an app full-screen from Mission Control by dragging it onto one of the Spaces at the top of the window.

Spaces

The top level of Mission Control contains Spaces, which are new Desktop areas into which you can group certain apps; e.g. the Apple productivity apps such as Pages and Numbers. This means that you can access these apps independently from other open items. This helps to organize your apps and files. To use Spaces:

 Move the cursor over the top right-hand corner of Mission Control and click on the **+** symbol

 A new **Space** is created along the top row of Mission Control

Desktop 2

 Drag an app onto the Space, and then any additional apps required

Desktop 2

4 The new Space can then be accessed by clicking on the Space within Mission Control, and all of the apps that have been placed here, or opened within the Space, will be available

5 macOS Apps

Apps are the programs with
which you start putting
macOS to use, either for
work or for fun. This chapter
looks at using apps and the
online App Store.

Launchpad

Even though the Dock can be used to store shortcuts to your applications, it is limited in terms of space. The full set of applications on your Mac can be found in the Finder (see Chapter 3) but macOS has a feature that allows you to quickly access and manage all of your applications. These include the ones that are pre-installed on your Mac and also any that you install yourself or download from the Apple App Store. This feature is called the Launchpad. To use it:

Hot tip

If the apps take up more than one screen, swipe from right to left with two fingers to view the additional pages, or click on the dots at the bottom of the window.

 Click once on this button on the Dock

Don't forget

To launch an app from within the Launchpad, click on it once.

 All of the apps (applications) are displayed

Hot tip

One of the apps in Utilities is Boot Camp Assistant, which can be used to run Windows on your Mac, if required.

 Similar types of apps can be grouped together in individual folders. By default, the **Other** (**Utilities**) apps are grouped in this way

4 To create a group of similar apps, drag the icon for one over another

  5 The apps are grouped together in a folder in the Launchpad, with a default name based on the type of app

6 To change the name, click on it once and overtype it with the new name

Don't forget

Most system apps – i.e. the ones that already come with your Mac – cannot be removed in the Launchpad, only ones you have downloaded. The exceptions are Pages, Numbers, Keynote, iMovie and GarageBand.

7 The folder appears within the **Launchpad** window

8 To remove an app, click and hold on it until it starts to jiggle and a cross appears. Click on the cross to remove it

Full-screen Apps

When working with apps we all like to be able to see as much of a window as possible. With macOS this is possible with the full-screen app option. This allows you to expand an app with this functionality so that it takes up the whole of your monitor or screen with a minimum of toolbars visible. Some apps have this functionality but some do not. To use full-screen apps:

1 By default, an app appears on the Desktop with other windows behind it

If the button in Step 2 is not visible then the app does not have the full-screen functionality.

2 Click on this button in the top left-hand corner of the app's window

3 The app is expanded to take up the whole window. The main Apple Menu bar and the Dock are hidden

...cont'd

4 To view the main Menu bar, move the cursor over the top of the screen

For more information about navigating with Multi-Touch Gestures, see pages 82-88.

5 You can move between all full-screen apps by swiping with three fingers left or right on a trackpad or Magic Mouse

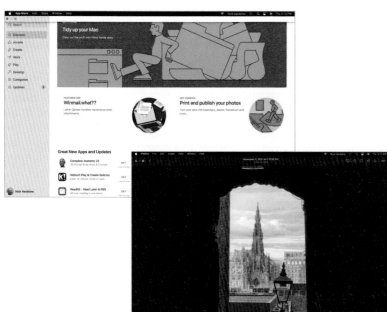

6 Move the cursor over the top left-hand corner of the screen and click on this button to close the full-screen functionality

7 In Mission Control all of the open full-screen apps are shown in the top row

macOS Apps

macOS apps include:

- **Books**. An app for downloading ebooks. (See pages 155-156.)

- **Calculator**. A basic calculator.

- **Calendar**. (See pages 106-107.)

- **Contacts**. (See pages 104-105.)

- **Dictionary**. A digital dictionary.

- **FaceTime**. Can be used for video calls. (See pages 138-142.)

- **Find My**. This can be used to locate missing Apple devices.

- **Home**. This can be used to control compatible smart home devices; e.g. smart lighting and smart heating.

- **Mail**. The default email app.

- **Maps**. For viewing locations and destinations worldwide.

- **Messages**. (See pages 134-136.)

- **Mission Control**. The function for organizing your Desktop.

- **Music, TV, Photos and Podcasts**. (See Chapter 8 for details about these apps.)

- **News**. This aggregates news stories from several sources. (See page 112.)

- **Notes**. (See pages 108-109.)

- **Photo Booth**. An app for creating photo effects.

- **Preview**. (See page 118.)

- **Reminders**. (See pages 110-111.)

- **Safari**. The macOS-specific web browser.

- **Stocks**. This can be used to display stock market information.

- **Time Machine**. macOS's backup facility.

- **Voice Memos**. (See page 113.)

- **Weather**. Provides international weather information.

The macOS apps can be accessed from the Launchpad and also the Applications folder from within the Finder.

Some apps are grouped together in the Utilities/Other folder. These include TextEdit, Chess, Stickies, Font Book, QuickTime Player, and Screenshot.

Macs with macOS also come with the Apple productivity apps, Pages (word processing), Numbers (spreadsheets) and Keynote (presentations). They are pre-installed and can also be downloaded, for free, from the App Store.

Accessing the App Store

The App Store is another macOS app. This is an online facility where you can download and buy new apps. These cover a range of categories such as Productivity, Business and Entertainment. When you select or buy an app from the App Store, it is downloaded automatically by the Launchpad and appears there next to the rest of the apps.

To buy apps from the App Store, you need to have an Apple ID. If you have not already set this up, it can be done when you first access the App Store. To use the App Store:

1 Click on this icon on the Dock or within the Launchpad

2 The Homepage of the App Store contains the current top featured and best new apps

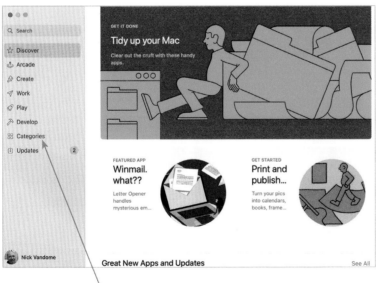

3 Your account information and quick links to other areas of the App Store are listed in the left-hand sidebar

Hot tip

You can set up an Apple ID when you first set up your Mac or you can do it when you first access the App Store.

Hot tip

Click on the **Arcade** button in the left-hand sidebar to access the Arcade option for playing games. This is a subscription service (with a one-month free trial) that gives unlimited access to original Apple games that can be played on your own or with other people. It can also be used with Family Sharing.

Don't forget

By default, the App Store opens at the Homepage, which is accessed by clicking on the **Discover** button in the left-hand sidebar.

Downloading Apps

The App Store contains a wide range of apps: from small, fun apps to powerful productivity ones. However, downloading them from the App Store is the same regardless of the type of app. The only differences are whether they need to be paid for or not and the length of time they take to download. To download an app from the App Store:

Hot tip

When downloading apps, start with a free one first so that you can get used to the process before you download paid-for apps.

1 Browse through the App Store until you find the required app

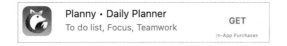

2 Click on the app to view a detailed description about it

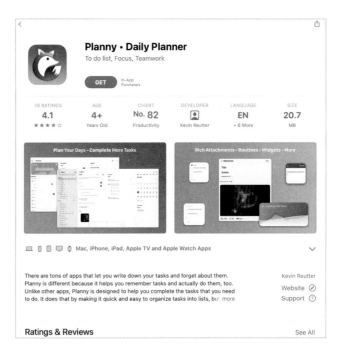

3 Click on the button next to the app icon to download it. If the app is free the button will say **Get**

4 If there is a charge (displayed in local currency) for the app, the button will say **Buy App** once the price is clicked

5 Click on the **Install** button

 INSTALL

6 Enter your **Apple ID** account details to continue downloading the app, then click on the **Get** button

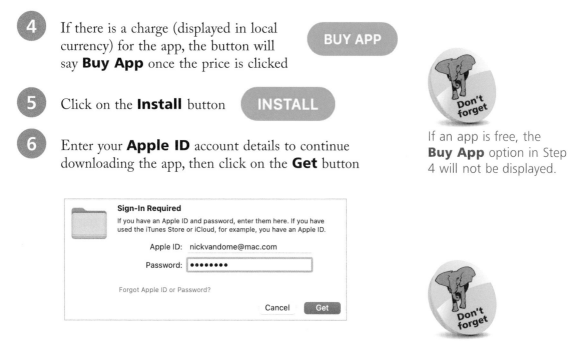

Sign-In Required
If you have an Apple ID and password, enter them here. If you have used the iTunes Store or iCloud, for example, you have an Apple ID.

Apple ID: nickvandome@mac.com

Password: ••••••••

Forgot Apple ID or Password?

Cancel   Get

7 The progress of the download is displayed in a progress bar underneath the Launchpad icon on the Dock

8 Once it has been downloaded, the app is available within the Launchpad

Siri

Mission Control

Entertainment

Planny

Don't forget

If an app is free, the **Buy App** option in Step 4 will not be displayed.

Don't forget

Depending on their size, different apps take differing amounts of time to be downloaded.

Don't forget

As you download more apps, additional pages will be created within the Launchpad to accommodate them.

Finding Apps

There are thousands of apps in the App Store, and sometimes the hardest task is locating the ones you want. However, there are a number of ways in which finding apps is made as easy as possible.

 Click on the **Discover** button

 The main window has a range of suggested apps. Scroll down the page to see a panel with the current **Top Free** apps and games

 Below this is a list of the current **Top Paid** apps and games

Top Charts has sections for paid-for apps and free ones.

 Click on the **See All** button to view a full list of **Top Charts** apps

5 Click on the buttons in the left-hand panel to view the available apps with them

6 Each heading contains relevant apps

Hot tip

Another way to find apps is to type a keyword into the Search box in the top left-hand corner of the App Store window.

101

7 Click on the **Categories** button

8 Browse through the apps by specific categories, such as Business, Entertainment and Finance

Managing Your Apps

Once you have bought apps from the App Store you can view details of ones you have purchased and also install updated versions of them. To view your purchased apps:

Don't forget

Even if you interrupt a download and turn off your Mac you will still be able to resume the download when you restart your computer.

Hot tip

Apps can also be updated automatically. This can be specified in **System Settings > General > Software Update**. Click on the **i** symbol next to **Automatic updates** and check **On** the **Download new updates when available** option.

1 Click on your own account name, in the bottom left-hand corner

2 Details of your purchased apps are displayed (including those that are free)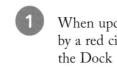

Updating apps

Improvements and fixes are being developed constantly, and these can be downloaded to ensure that all of your apps are up-to-date.

1 When updates are available this is indicated by a red circle on the App Store icon on the Dock

2 Click on the **Updates** button

3 Information about the update is displayed next to the app that is due to be updated

4 Click on the **Update** button to update an individual app

5 Click on the **Update All** button to update all apps that are due to be updated

102

6 Getting Productive

There are several built-in apps within macOS that can be used to create, store and display information for use every day. This chapter shows how to access and use these apps so that you can make the most of macOS as an effective and efficient productivity tool.

Contacts (Address Book)

The Contacts app can be used to store contact information, which can then be used in different apps and shared via iCloud. To view contacts:

Hot tip

Contacts can be shared by clicking on the **Share** button and selecting one of the available options.

✉	Email Card
💬	Message Card
📶	AirDrop Card
📝	Notes
⋯	More...

1 Open **Contacts** from this address book icon, and click on one of the contacts in the left-hand panel to view their details

Adding contact information

The main function of the Contacts app is to store details of personal and business contacts. Contacts must be added manually for each entry, but it can prove to be a valuable resource once this has been completed. To add contact information:

Hot tip

Click on the **Edit** button to edit a contact's details.

Edit

1 Click on this button to add a new contact   +

2 Click on a category, and enter contact information. Press the **Tab** key to move to the next field

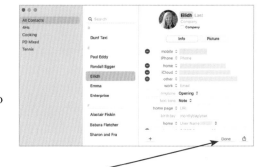

3 Click on the **Done** button once you have completed the entry

Creating lists

In addition to creating individual entries in the Contacts app, group contacts can also be created, using the list option. This is a way of grouping contacts with similar interests or connections. Once a list has been created, all of the entries within it can be accessed and contacted by selecting the relevant entry in the left-hand panel. To create a list:

Don't forget

Individuals can be included in several lists. If you change their details in one list, these changes will take effect across all lists in which the entry occurs.

1 Select **File** > **New List** from the Menu bar to create a new list entry

2 Give the new list a name

3 Drag individual entries into the list (the individual entries are retained, too)

Hot tip

Lists in the Contacts app can be used to send group emails; i.e. you can type the name of a group into the **To:** box to generate names in the list, and then send an email to all of these recipients.

4 Click on a list name to view the members of the group

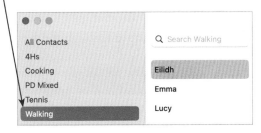

Calendar

Electronic calendars are now a standard part of modern life, and with macOS this function is performed by the Calendar app. Not only can this be used on your Mac; it can also be synchronized with other Apple devices such as an iPad or an iPhone, using iCloud. To create a calendar:

Click on the **Today** button to view the current day. Click on the Forward or Back arrows to move to the next day, week, month or year, depending on what is selected in Step 2.

 1 Click on this icon on the Dock or in the Launchpad

 2 Select whether to view the calendar by Day, Week, Month or Year

Day	Week	**Month**	Year

3 In Month view, the current day is denoted by a red circle on the date

If Family Sharing has been activated, the Family calendar will automatically be added for all members of the Family Sharing group.

4 Scroll up and down to move through the weeks and months. In macOS this is done with continuous scrolling, which means you can view weeks across different months; i.e. you can view the second half of one month and the first half of the next one in the same window

Adding events

1 Select a date and double-click on it; or **Ctrl + click** on the date, then select **New Event**

2 Click on the **New Event** field and enter an event name

3 Click on the date or time to amend it by entering new details. Check **On** the **all-day:** box to set the event for a whole day

Click on this button on the Menu bar to add a **Quick Event**, with just one text box for all of the relevant information. Once it has been added it can then be edited like a regular event by double-clicking on it.

Finding locations

When adding events you can also find details about locations.

1 Click on the **Add Location or Video Call** field, and start typing a destination name or zip (postal) code. Suggestions will appear underneath, including matching items from your contacts list. Click on a location to select it

Other items that can be included in an event are: inviting people to it; calculating the travel time from your current location; creating a repeat event; and setting an alert for it.

2 A map of the location is displayed, including a real-time weather summary for the location. Click on the map to view it in greater detail in the **Maps** app

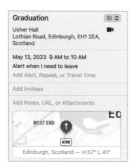

Taking Notes

It is always useful to have a quick way of making notes of everyday things such as shopping lists, recipes or packing lists for traveling. With macOS, the Notes app is perfect for this task. To use it:

1 Click on this icon on the Dock or in the Launchpad

2 The right-hand panel is where notes are created. The middle panel displays a list of all notes

The first line of a note becomes its heading in the notes panel.

3 Click on this button on the top toolbar to view the Notes Homepage as a gallery of thumbnails, rather than the default list option. This makes it easier to identify specific lists and their content

Ctrl + click on a note in the middle panel and click on the **Pin Note** option, to pin the note at the top of the panel.

4 Click on this button to add a new note

5 As more notes are added, the most recent appears at the top of the list in the middle panel (below any notes that have been pinned). Double-click the new note to add text and edit formatting options (see the next page)

Today

New Note
10:29 AM No additional text
Notes

Shopping
10:11 AM Grapes
Notes

Formatting notes

In macOS there are a number of formatting options for the Notes app.

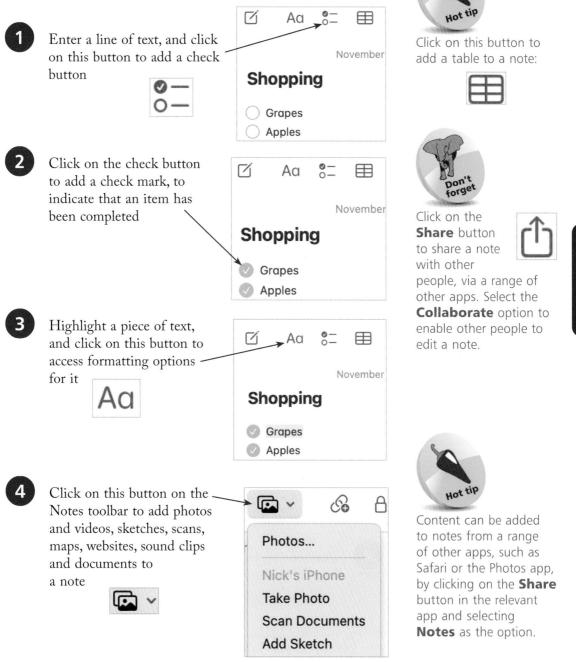

1 Enter a line of text, and click on this button to add a check button

2 Click on the check button to add a check mark, to indicate that an item has been completed

3 Highlight a piece of text, and click on this button to access formatting options for it

4 Click on this button on the Notes toolbar to add photos and videos, sketches, scans, maps, websites, sound clips and documents to a note

Hot tip

Click on this button to add a table to a note:

Don't forget

Click on the **Share** button to share a note with other people, via a range of other apps. Select the **Collaborate** option to enable other people to edit a note.

Hot tip

Content can be added to notes from a range of other apps, such as Safari or the Photos app, by clicking on the **Share** button in the relevant app and selecting **Notes** as the option.

109

Setting Reminders

Another useful app for keeping organized is Reminders. This enables you to create lists for different topics and also set reminders for specific items. A date and time can be set for each reminder, and when this is reached, the reminder appears on your Mac screen (and in the Notification Center). To use Reminders:

1 Click on this icon on the Dock or in the Launchpad

2 The Reminders window contains a **My Lists** section where lists and reminders are created and a **Smart Lists** section, at the top of the left-hand sidebar, where matching items are collated

110

3 Click on the one of the **My Lists** options; e.g. **Reminders**

4 Click on this button to add a new reminder

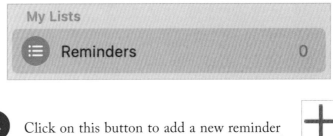

5 Enter the title of the reminder and click on the **i** button to access the **Details** window

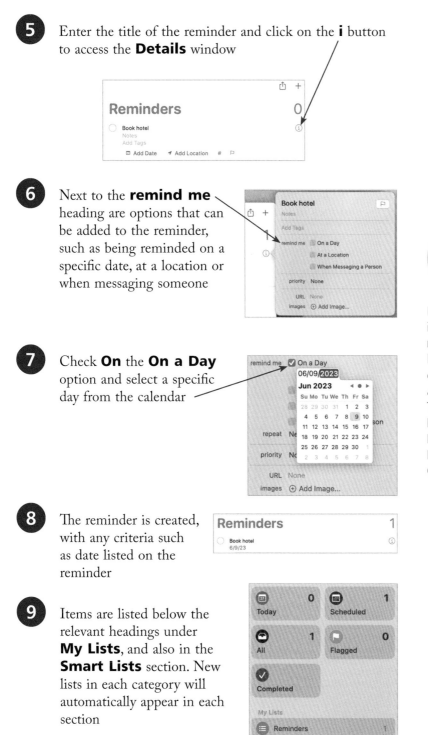

6 Next to the **remind me** heading are options that can be added to the reminder, such as being reminded on a specific date, at a location or when messaging someone

7 Check **On** the **On a Day** option and select a specific day from the calendar

8 The reminder is created, with any criteria such as date listed on the reminder

9 Items are listed below the relevant headings under **My Lists**, and also in the **Smart Lists** section. New lists in each category will automatically appear in each section

111

Hot tip

If the **On a Day** option is selected in Step 7, a **repeat** option then becomes available. This can be used to create a recurring reminder. The options for this are **None**, **Every Day**, **Every Week**, **Every Month**, **Every Year**, or **Custom**.

News

The News app has been a regular feature on Apple's mobile devices for a number of years. It is also available on Macs using macOS. To use it:

1 Click on the **News** app

2 Click on the **Today** button in the left-hand panel to view the latest stories in your news feed

Hot tip

Click on the **News+** button in the left-hand sidebar to access the subscription service for Apple News.

3 On the News app Menu bar, select **File > Discover Channels...** to view subjects or publications that you are following; i.e. they are used to populate your news feed

4 In the **Channels** section, click on items to select them and add the topics or publications as favorites on your **Today** page

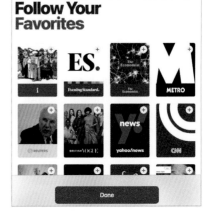

Voice Memos

Voice memos are an increasingly popular way to send short voice messages to family and friends. They can also be used as a method of verbal note-taking, when you want to remember something. To use voice memos:

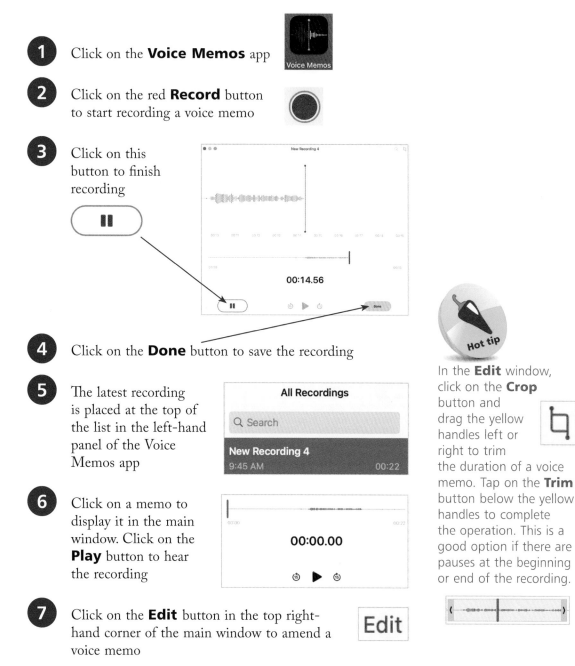

1 Click on the **Voice Memos** app

2 Click on the red **Record** button to start recording a voice memo

3 Click on this button to finish recording

00:14.56

4 Click on the **Done** button to save the recording

5 The latest recording is placed at the top of the list in the left-hand panel of the Voice Memos app

All Recordings

Q Search

New Recording 4
9:45 AM   00:22

6 Click on a memo to display it in the main window. Click on the **Play** button to hear the recording

00:00.00

7 Click on the **Edit** button in the top right-hand corner of the main window to amend a voice memo

Edit

Hot tip

In the **Edit** window, click on the **Crop** button and drag the yellow handles left or right to trim the duration of a voice memo. Tap on the **Trim** button below the yellow handles to complete the operation. This is a good option if there are pauses at the beginning or end of the recording.

Getting Around with Maps

With the **Maps** app you need never again wonder about where a location is, or worry about getting directions to somewhere. Using **Maps** in macOS, you will be able to do the following:

● Search maps from around the world

● Find addresses

● Find famous buildings or landmarks

● Get directions between different locations

● View transit information for a route

● View traffic conditions

Viewing maps

Enable **Location Services** and then you can start looking around maps, from the viewpoint of your current location.

Don't forget

Location Services can be enabled in **System Settings** > **Privacy & Security**. Under **Privacy**, click on **Location Services** and check **On** the **Location Services** checkbox. Maps can be used without Location Services but this would mean that Maps cannot use your current location or determine information in relation to this.

1 Click on this icon on the Dock or in the Launchpad

2 Click on this button to view your current location

3 Double-click to zoom in on the map. Press **Option + double-click** to zoom out. Or, swipe outward with thumb and forefinger to zoom in, and pinch inward to zoom out

4 Click on this button to show or hide the left-hand sidebar

Finding locations

Locations in Maps can be found for addresses, cities or landmarks.
To find items in Maps:

1 Enter a term into the Search box and click on one of the results

2 The selected item is displayed and shown on a map with a panel displaying information about it. You can also access a **Flyover Tour** of the location (if available)

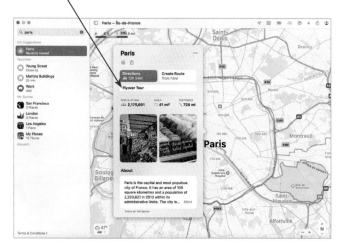

3 Click on this button on the top toolbar to select **Explore**, **Driving**, **Transit** or **Satellite** views of the location

Don't forget

Flyover Tour (if available for a location) provides an animated 3D experience that travels through the most notable sights for that location.

Hot tip

Click on the **3D** button on the top toolbar to change the perspective of the map being viewed. Rotate your fingers on the trackpad to change the orientation of the map.

...cont'd

Getting directions

Within Maps you can also get directions to most locations.

1 Search for a location and click on the **Directions** button

2 By default, your current location is used for the start of the route. If you want to change this, click here and enter a new location. Click on one of the options at the top of the panel for reaching your destination (**Drive, Walk, Transit** or **Cycle**). Click on one of the route options

Click on the **Share** button on the top toolbar to send directions to a mobile device, such as an iPhone or an iPad, so that you can follow the directions on the go.

3 The route is shown on the map with the directions. The default mode of transport is for driving

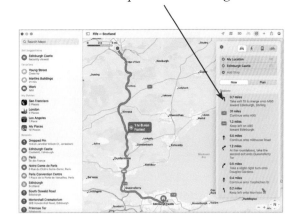

4 From the options in Step 3 on page 115, click on the **Driving** button to view traffic conditions for the selected route

Finding transit directions

In macOS there is an option for accessing transit options between two locations. To do this:

1 Enter the two locations, as shown on the previous page. Click on the **Transit** button

2 The transit options are shown in a panel on the map. Click here next to an option to view its full details. This will include any parts of the journey where you will have to walk between the transit services required for your journey

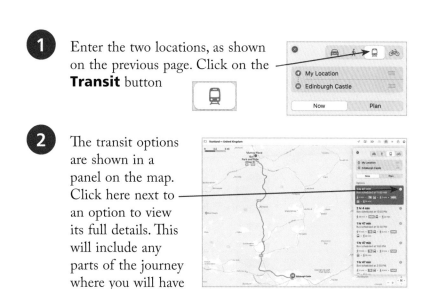

Look Around

If a specific street is being viewed, there is an option to view it with a photographic interface, from where you can explore the location and move around the area. To do this:

1 Access a street location and click on this icon on the top toolbar

2 A **Look Around** window is activated over the map. Click within the Look Around window to move through the location, or click on this icon to move its location on the map

Hot tip

Click on the **Plan** button in Step 2 to view the transit details for a specific date and time.

Beware

The **Transit** option is only available for a limited number of locations around the world – the majority being in the US.

117

Preview

Preview is a macOS app that can be used to view multiple file types, particularly image file formats. This can be useful if you just want to view documents without editing them in a dedicated app, such as an image-editing app. Preview in macOS can also be used to store and view documents in iCloud.

To open Preview, click on this icon in the **Applications** folder in the Finder, on the Dock or in the Launchpad:

Preview

1 Open **Preview** and click on one of the options in the Finder sidebar

Preview is also a good option for viewing Portable Document Format (PDF) documents.

2 Double-click on an item to view it at full size. This can be from any of the folders within the Finder. The item is opened in the Preview window. Use the Preview toolbar to manage and edit open items

Printing

macOS makes the printing process as simple as possible, partly by its ability to automatically install new printers as soon as they are connected to your Mac. However, it is also possible to install printers manually. To do this:

1 Open **System Settings** and click on the **Printers & Scanners** option

Printers & Scanners

2 Click on the **Add Printer, Scanner, or Fax...** button to add a new printer

3 Select an available printer

4 Click on the **Add** button to load the printer drivers (printer software) for the selected printer

For most printers, macOS will detect them when they are first connected, and they should be ready to use without the need to install any software or apply new settings.

5 The printer drivers for operating the printer are added. The printer is added in the **Printers & Scanners** window, under the **Printers** list, ready for use

Once a printer has been installed, documents can be printed by selecting **File** > **Print** from the Menu bar. Print settings can be set at this point, and they can also be set by selecting **File** > **Page/Print Setup** from the Menu bar in most apps.

macOS Utilities

In addition to the apps in the **Applications** folder, there are also a number of utility apps that perform a variety of tasks within macOS. (Some of the utilities vary depending on the hardware setup of your Mac.) The utility apps are in the **Other** folder.

The **Utilities** folder is also available from within the **Applications** folder. On some systems it may appear as "**Other**" in the Launchpad.

Other

1 Access the Launchpad to access the **Other** folder. The utilities are displayed within the Other folder

The utilities are the workhorses of macOS. They do not have the glamour of apps such as the Music app, but they perform vital gathering of information and general maintenance tasks.

- **Activity Monitor**. This contains information about the system memory being used and disk activity (see page 180 for more details).

- **AirPort Utility**. This sets up the AirPort wireless networking facility that can be used to connect to the internet with a Wi-Fi connection (pre-2018).

- **Audio MIDI Setup**. This can be used for adding audio devices and setting their properties.

- **Automator**. This can be used to create automated tasks.

- **Bluetooth File Exchange**. This determines how files are exchanged between your computer and other Bluetooth devices (if this function is enabled).

- **Boot Camp Assistant**. This can be used to run Windows operating systems on your Mac.

- **Chess**. A game that can be played against your Mac.

- **ColorSync Utility**. This can be used to view and create color profiles on your computer. These can then be used by apps to try to match output color with monitor color.

You may never need to use a utility like the Console app, but it is worth having a look at it just to see the inner workings of a computer.

- **Console**. This displays behind-the-scenes messages that are passed around the computer while its usual tasks are being performed.

- **Digital Color Meter**. This can be used to measure the exact color values of a particular color.

- **Disk Utility**. This can be used to view details about attached disks and repair errors (see page 178 for more details).

- **Feedback Assistant**. This can be used to receive and send feedback updates about Apple and macOS.

- **Font Book**. This displays the available system fonts.

- **Grapher**. This is a utility for creating simple or more complex scientific graphs.

- **Image Capture**. This can be used to capture images, or transfer and scan images.

- **Keychain Access**. This can be used to manage passwords for websites and also create new secure passwords as required.

- **Migration Assistant**. This helps in the transfer of files between two Mac computers. This can be used if you buy a new Mac and you need to transfer files from another one.

- **QuickTime Player**. This can be used to play video files.

- **Screenshot**. This is a utility that can be used to capture screenshots, which are images of the screen at a given point in time. You can grab different portions of the screen, including timed options.

- **Script Editor**. This can be used to create your own scripts with Apple's dedicated scripting app, AppleScript.

- **Shortcuts**. This can be used to create automated actions.

- **Stickies**. This can be used to attach short notes to the screen.

- **System Information**. This contains details of the hardware devices and software applications that are installed on your computer (see page 179 for more details).

- **Terminal**. Within the Terminal you can view the workings of UNIX and also start to write your own apps, if you have some UNIX programming knowledge.

- **TextEdit**. This is a basic word processing app.

- **Time Machine**. This is the macOS backup facility.

- **VoiceOver Utility**. This has various options for the digital voice that can be used to read out what is on the screen, and it is particularly useful for users who are visually impaired.

Hot tip

The **Screenshot** utility is a feature that is useful if you are producing manuals or books, and need to display examples of a screen or app.

Creating PDF Documents

Portable Document Format (PDF) is a file format that preserves the formatting of an original document, and it can also be viewed on a variety of computer platforms including Mac, Windows and UNIX. macOS has a built-in PDF function that can produce PDF files from many apps. To use this:

1 Open a file in an app and select **File > Export as PDF...**, or use the **File > Save As** option and change the format of the document to PDF, where offered

2 Browse to a destination for the file, and click on the **Save** button

3 Locate the selected destination to view and open the newly-created PDF file. You can then access options for viewing, sharing or marking up the document

7 Internet and Communication

This chapter shows how to get the most out of the internet and keeping in touch. It covers how to use the macOS web browser, Safari, and its email app, Mail. It also covers Messages for text messaging, and video calling with the updated FaceTime app.

Before you connect to the internet you must have an Internet Service Provider (ISP) who will provide you with the relevant method of connection; e.g. cable, wireless or dial-up (if being used). They will also provide you with any passwords (for connecting to a Wi-Fi router) and login details. Click on the **Network** option in System Settings to view the available networks.

If the Favorites Bar is not visible, select **View** from the Menu bar and check on the **Show Favorites Bar** option. From this menu you can also select or deselect items such as showing the sidebar, the Status Bar and the Reading List. You can also display the sidebar by clicking on this button:

About Safari

Safari is a web browser that is designed specifically to be used with macOS. It is similar in most respects to other browsers, but it usually functions more quickly with macOS.

Safari overview

 Click here on the Dock to launch Safari

 All of the controls are at the top of the browser

Toolbar   Address Bar/Search Box   Tabs

Favorites Bar   Main content area

Address Bar/Search Box
In Safari, the Address Bar and the Search Box are combined, and can be used for searching for an item or entering a web address to go to that page.

1 Click in the Address Bar/Search Box

2 Type a website address or a keyword. As you type, suggestions appear below the Address Bar/Search Box. Click on the **Top Hit** option to go to that website

Start Page

When you first open Safari or open a new tab, the Start page is displayed. This can contain a selection of items that can be set within the Safari settings. The options include favorites, frequently-visited pages and items selected by Siri, but the items displayed can be modified (see pages 126-127). To use the Start page:

1 The Start page is displayed when Safari is opened or when a new tab is opened (unless specified differently; see the second Hot tip on page 127)

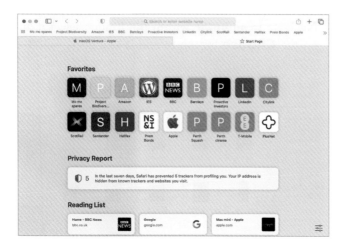

2 Swipe up the Start page to view the available options

Safari is a full-screen app and can be expanded by clicking the green button in the top left-hand corner. For more information on full-screen apps, see pages 94-95.

125

Move the cursor over the Favorites section on the Start page and click on the **Show All** button to view more favorite pages. Move the cursor over the Favorites section again and click on the **Show Less** button to reduce the number of visible items.

...cont'd

Hot tip

The **Show iCloud Tabs** option for the Start page displays open tabs in Safari from other Apple devices, such as an iPhone or an iPad, provided that they are using the same Apple ID.

 Ctrl + click anywhere on the Start page to access the menu for displaying items. Check items **On** or **Off** as required

✓ Show Favorites
  Show Frequently Visited
✓ Show Privacy Report
✓ Show Siri Suggestions
✓ Show Reading List
✓ Show Shared with You
✓ Show iCloud Tabs

Choose Background...

 Click on the **Choose Background...** option to select a background image for the Start page

5 Navigate to an image within the Finder, select it and click on the **Choose** button to add it as a background

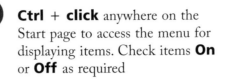

6 The background image is added to the Start page, behind the existing elements on the page

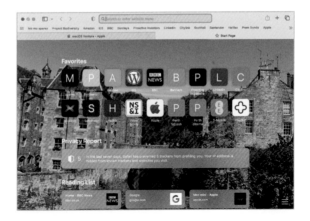

7 One of the options for displaying on the Start page is a **Privacy Report**, which can be used to show certain security issues with pages in Safari

8 Click on the Privacy Report on the Start page to view full details for a 30-day period of using Safari, for elements that track your actions across websites

Items that appear in new windows or tabs can be customized with the Safari settings. To do this:

1 Select **Safari > Settings...** from the Safari Menu bar

2 Click on the **General** tab for accessing options for how new windows and tabs open

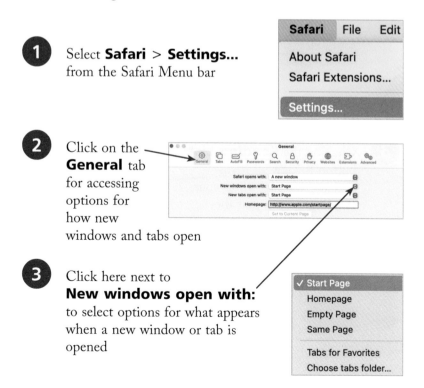

3 Click here next to **New windows open with:** to select options for what appears when a new window or tab is opened

Safari Sidebar

A useful feature in Safari is the Safari sidebar. This is a panel in which you can view all of your bookmarks and Reading List items, which can be read when the Mac is offline.

Hot tip

Click on this button in the top right-hand corner of the sidebar to access options for managing groups of tabs. The options include **New Empty Tab Group** and **New Tab Group with [] Tabs**, which creates a new tab group using the existing open tabs. Different tab groups can be used to open related web pages within the same group, to keep related subjects together.

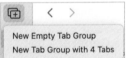

1 Select **View** > **Show Sidebar** from the Safari Menu bar, or click on this button on the top toolbar

2 Click on the **Bookmarks** button to view all items that you have bookmarked (see page 130)

3 Click on the **Reading List** button to view all items that you have added to your Reading List so that they can be read later, even if you are offline and not connected to the internet. These can be added from the **Share** button on the top toolbar

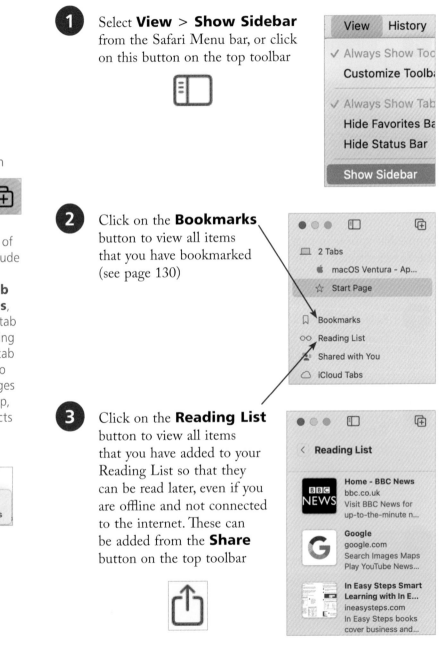

128

Safari Tabbed Browsing

Tabs are now a familiar feature on web browsers, so you can have multiple sites open within the same browser window.

 1 When more than one tab is open, the tabs appear at the top of the web pages

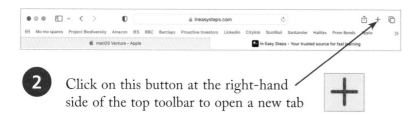

2 Click on this button at the right-hand side of the top toolbar to open a new tab

3 Select one of the options from the Start page, or enter a keyword or phrase, or website address, in the Address Bar/ Search Box

4 Click on this button next to the **New Tab** button to minimize all of the current tabs

5 Scroll up and down the window to view all open tabs in thumbnail view. Click on one to view it at full size. Click on this button to open a new tab

Don't forget

Select **Safari > Settings > Tabs** from the Menu bar to specify settings for the way tabs in Safari operate. Click on the **Separate** button to display the tabs bar in the traditional format. Click on the **Compact** button to display the tabs separately, above the Favorites bar. This also enables the color of the web page being viewed to extend to the top of the window.

Don't forget

If you have open tabs on other Apple devices (e.g. other Mac computers, iPads or iPhones) these will be listed if you select to open a new tab in Step 5. Click on an item to open it in Safari on your Mac.

Adding Bookmarks

Bookmarks is a feature with which you can create quick links to your favorite web pages or the ones you visit most frequently. Bookmarks can be added to a menu or the Bookmarks panel in Safari, which makes them even quicker to access. Folders can also be created to store less frequently-used bookmarks. To view and create bookmarks:

1 Click on this button to view the sidebar

2 Access the **Bookmarks** section as shown on page 128 to view the currently-available bookmarks and any bookmarks folders

Hot tip

Bookmarks can be added to the Favorites Bar, which can be displayed at the top of the Safari window, below the Address Bar. To add bookmarks to the Favorites Bar, select **Favorites** for **Add this page to:** in Step 4. To show (or hide) the Favorites Bar, select **View > Show Favorites Bar** (or **Hide Favorites Bar**) from the Safari Menu bar. The Favorites folder is displayed at the top of the Bookmarks panel.

3 Click on the **Share** button on the top toolbar, and click on the **Add Bookmark** button to create a bookmark for the page currently being viewed

4 Enter a name for the bookmark and select a location for it

5 Click on the **Add** button

Website Settings

One of the most annoying things about using the web is the adverts that seem to appear by coincidence when you are browsing a website. These are actually based on items that you have previously looked at on the web, and are generated by cookies that have been downloaded from the original site. However, with macOS a lot of these adverts are blocked automatically, and you can also apply your own settings for specific pages to enable or restrict certain items. To do this:

1 Select **Safari** > **Settings for [website name]** from the Safari Menu bar

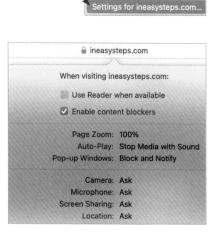

2 Make selections as required, such as enabling the Reader function and using content blockers. Check **On** the **Enable content blockers** option to block unwanted items

The Reader function is one where a web page can be read without additional items such as toolbars, buttons and navigation bars. If a page supports the Reader function it will display this button in the Address Bar:

3 Select **Safari** > **Settings** from the Safari Menu bar, and click on the **Privacy** button on the top toolbar

4 Under **Website tracking:**, check **On** the **Prevent cross-site tracking** checkbox to prevent websites from displaying adverts based on what you have viewed on other sites

Mail

Email is an essential element for most computer users, and Macs come with their own email app called Mail. This covers all the email functionality that most people could need.

When first using Mail, you have to set up your email account. This can be done with most email accounts and also a wide range of webmail accounts, including iCloud. To add email accounts:

Don't forget

Mail is a full-screen app. For more information on full-screen apps, see pages 94-95.

Don't forget

You can set up more than one account in the Mail app and you can download messages from all of the accounts that you set up. To set up an account from the Mail app, select **Mail** > **Add Account** from the Menu bar.

Hot tip

Since the release of macOS Ventura, it is possible to unsend an email if it has been sent in error, although this may not work if the recipient is using an earlier version of macOS. To unsend an email, click on the **Undo Send** button at the bottom of the Mail Inbox panel once an email has been sent, for up to 10 seconds.

⟳ Undo Send

132

1 Click on this icon on the Dock

2 Check **On** the button next to the type of account that you want to add to the Mail app; e.g. if you have an iCloud account, select **iCloud** to add this

3 Enter details of the account, and click on the **Next** button

4 Check the **Mail** option **On** for iCloud to sync your iCloud email across any other Apple devices and also your online account at **www.icloud.com** Click on the **Add Account** button

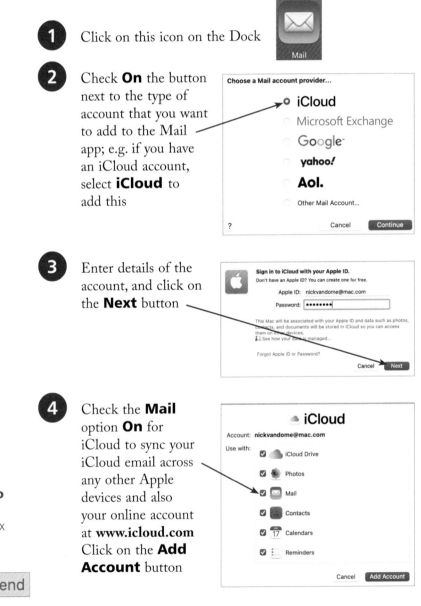

Using Mail

Mail enables you to send and receive emails, and also format them to your own style. This can be simply formatting text, or attaching images or documents. To use Mail:

 Click on the **Get Mail** button to download available email messages

 Click on the **New Message** button to create a new email

3 Click on these buttons to **Reply** to, **Reply** (to) **All**, or **Forward** an email you have received

4 Select or open an email, and click on the **Trash** button to delete it

5 Click on the **Junk** button to mark an email as junk or spam. This trains Mail to identify junk mail. After a period of time, these types of messages will automatically be moved straight into the Junk mailbox

6 Click on the **Format** button to access options for formatting the text in an email

7 Use these buttons in the New Message window to select fonts and font size; color; bold; italic; underlining; strikethrough; and alignment options

8 Click on the **Attach** button to browse your folders, to include a file in your email. This can be items such as photos, Word documents or PDF files

Hot tip

To show descriptive text underneath an icon in Mail, **Ctrl** + **click** next to an icon and select **Icon and Text** from the menu.

Hot tip

When entering the name of a recipient for a message, Mail will display details of matching names from the Contacts app. For instance, if you type "DA", all of the entries in your Contacts app beginning with this will be displayed, and you can then select the required one.

Hot tip

If you forward an email with an attachment, then the attachment is included. If you reply to an email, the attachment will not be included.

Messaging

The Messages app enables you to send text messages (iMessages) to other macOS users or those with an iPhone or iPad using iOS or iPadOS. It can also be used to send photos and videos. To use Messages:

Don't forget

iMessages are specific to Apple and sent over Wi-Fi. Short Message Service (SMS) messages are usually sent between cellular devices, such as smartphones, that are contracted to a compatible mobile services provider. SMS messages can also be sent with the Messages app, to Apple or non-Apple users.

1 Click on this icon on the Dock

2 Click on this button to start a new conversation

3 Click on this button and select a contact (this will be from your Contacts app)

To send an iMessage, the recipient must have an Apple ID

4 The person with whom you are having a conversation is displayed in the left-hand panel. The conversation continues down the right-hand panel

Hot tip

Audio messages can also be included in an iMessage. Click on this icon to the right of the text box, and record your message:

5 Click in the text box at the bottom of the main panel to write a message, and press **Return** on the keyboard to send

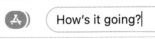

6 Click on this button at the right-hand side of the text box to access a range of emojis (small graphical symbols)

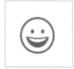

7 Click on an emoji to add it to a message

8 Scroll left and right of the window to view all of the emojis available, or click on the bottom toolbar to move through the categories

Messages in macOS also supports Tapback, whereby you can add an icon to a message as a quick reply. To do this, click and hold on a message text and click on an icon.

9 Some emojis of people have options to select different styles. Click and hold on a relevant item to view the options. Click on one to add it to a message

Pinning conversations

It is possible to keep your favorite conversations at the top of the left-hand panel by pinning them there. To do this:

1 **Ctrl + click** on a conversation in the left-hand panel and click on the **Pin** option

2 The conversation is pinned at the top of the panel

Hot tip

Photos and videos can also be added to messages, from the **Photos** option in Step 2.

Beware

The image in Step 5 is the basis for a Memoji, but it is not available on its own. Instead, variations are available; see Step 6.

...cont'd

Adding Memojis

Memojis are customized graphics that can be added to an iMessage in a similar way to an emoji. However, Memoji categories can also be created based on your own design, which can include a Memoji of yourself. To do this:

1 Click on this icon next to the text box

2 Click on the **Memoji Stickers** option

3 Click on the items on the top toolbar to view the different categories of Memoji. Click on a Memoji to add it to a message

4 Click on this button in the top left-hand corner of the Memoji window to create a new, customized, Memoji category

5 A plain avatar for the Memoji is displayed in the main window. The left-hand sidebar contains categories for customizing the face. For each category, specific options appear below the face. Click on one to add it

6 Add items to the avatar as required, using the categories in the left-hand sidebar. Click on the **Done** button to complete the Memoji, which is added to the Memoji Stickers panel

Editing and Unsending iMessages

When sending text iMessages from a Mac (using macOS Ventura or a later version) it is now possible to edit messages with any typos or mistakes in them, and also unsend a message if it has been sent in error or contains something that you didn't mean to include, although there is a time limit for these operations.

Editing an iMessage

1 **Ctrl + click** on a message once it has been sent and click on the **Edit** button

Just testing something - ignore this!

Delivered

Edit

2 Edit the message as required and click on this icon (the check mark symbol)

Just testing something!

✓

Delivered

3 The edited text is displayed in the conversation window

Just testing something!

Edited

Unsending an iMessage

1 **Ctrl + click** on a message once it has been sent and click on the **Undo Send** button

Undo Send

2 A message is displayed to indicate that the message has been unsent

Today 15:33

You unsent a message. Lucy may still see the message on devices where the software hasn't been updated.

Don't forget

iMessages can be edited up to five times within 15 minutes of them being sent. They can be unsent within two minutes of being sent.

Beware

Editing and unsending iMessages is only effective if they are sent to other people using macOS Ventura (or iOS 16 for an iPhone and iPadOS 16 for an iPad). If not, the editing and unsending operations may not work and the recipient will just see the original message.

Video Chatting with FaceTime

Video chatting is a very personal and interactive way to keep in touch with family and friends around the world. To use FaceTime for video chatting:

Don't forget

To make video calls with FaceTime you need an active internet connection and to be signed in with your Apple ID.

1 Click on the **FaceTime** app

2 Click on the **New FaceTime** button

3 Enter the name of a contact (or select one of the **Suggested** options)

Hot tip

When you receive a FaceTime call, click on the **Accept** button to connect the call. Click on the **Decline** button to refuse it, or click on the down-pointing arrow next to the Decline button to select an option for replying to the invite or to set a reminder.

| Accept ˅ |
| Decline ˅ |
| Reply with Message... |
| Remind Me in 5 Minutes |
| Remind Me in 15 Minutes |
| Remind Me in 1 Hour |

4 Click on the **FaceTime** button to make a FaceTime call (to another FaceTime user: the **Create Link** button in Step 2 can be used to make FaceTime calls to non-FaceTime users; see page 140)

5 When you have connected, your contact appears in the main window and you appear in a Picture in Picture thumbnail in the corner. Click and drag your own thumbnail to move it around the screen. The orientation of the FaceTime window depends on the one being used by the other person on the call

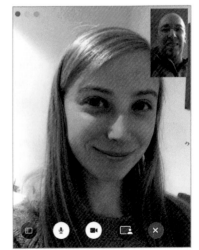

6 Use these buttons during a call to, from left to right: access the FaceTime sidebar (see the next step); mute or unmute the microphone; turn the camera on or off for the call (audio will still be available if the camera is off); use SharePlay (see pages 141-142); and end the call

7 Click on the FaceTime sidebar button in Step 6 to access more options for the call, including, from top to bottom: adding more people to the call; sharing links to the call for non-FaceTime users; and silencing requests to join FaceTime calls to which you are invited

The **Share Link** option in Step 7 can be used to create FaceTime calls with non-FaceTime users, including those using the Windows and Android operating systems. See page 140 for details.

Microphone modes

FaceTime also has options for how the microphone operates.

1 Start a FaceTime call, access the Control Center (see pages 34-35) and click on the **Mic Mode** button

2 Click on the **Voice Isolation** button to block out background noise and give clearer prominence to the current speaker in a call

Spatial sound is used in group calls to present the sound as coming from the direction of the screen in which someone's FaceTime window is positioned, to create a more natural effect.

...cont'd

Creating a FaceTime link

Before macOS Monterey was released in October 2021, it was only possible to use FaceTime to make video calls to other FaceTime users, using an Apple device. However, that has now changed and the functionality of FaceTime has been expanded considerably, with the inclusion of an option to send a link to anyone, who can then join the FaceTime call via the web. To do this:

Don't forget

It is also possible to invite someone to an existing FaceTime call, via a link, using the **Share Link** button in Step 7 on page 139.

1 Open the FaceTime app and click on the **Create Link** button

2 Select an option for how you want to send the link to join the FaceTime call; e.g. by email

Don't forget

When someone receives an invitation to a FaceTime call, the recipient can tap once on the **FaceTime Link** button in the invitation, enter their name and tap once on the **Continue** button.

3 Compose an invitation in the app selected in Step 2 and send it to the recipient

Using SharePlay in FaceTime

SharePlay is a function within FaceTime that enables you to share your screen and to play movies and TV shows, or play music, and share this content with other people on a FaceTime call. To do this:

 Within the FaceTime app, select **FaceTime** > **Settings** from the top Menu bar. Click on the **SharePlay** tab and check **On** the **SharePlay** checkbox

Start a FaceTime call and click on this button on the FaceTime control panel to share your Mac screen with everyone else on an existing call

Click on the **Share My Screen** button

Share My Screen

When a screen is being shared in a FaceTime call with SharePlay, whatever is shown on the sharing screen will be visible on everyone else's screen too. This appears as a separate panel, and the user's video feed is automatically turned off

Don't forget

Content for SharePlay is synchronized for everyone in a FaceTime call so that everyone sees and hears the same content at the same time.

Hot tip

If content is being shared with SharePlay from the TV app, all participants can use the TV app controls; e.g. everyone can pause/play, rewind or fast forward, and this will be applied for everyone in the call.

Hot tip

The controls at the top of the window in Step 4 can be used to make the content full-screen and adjust the volume. This only affects the device on which the changes are being made, not everyone in the call.

...cont'd

Sharing music, movies or TV shows

SharePlay can also be used to share content with other people on a FaceTime call from the Music app and the TV app. To do this:

1 Start a FaceTime call and open either the **Music** app or the **TV** app. For either one, open the item you want to share on the FaceTime call

2 For music, click on the **SharePlay** button and select how you want to start sharing music each time

3 For the **TV** app, select how you want to use an item you are opening; i.e. use it with SharePlay so that people on the FaceTime call can see it, or just open it for yourself on your Mac

4 Content from the **TV** app that is used with SharePlay plays within the FaceTime interface and everyone on the call will be able to view it

8 Digital Lifestyle

Leisure time, and how we use it, is a significant issue for everyone. This chapter details some of the options with macOS, including photos, music, movies and reading books.

Using the Photos App

The **Photos** app is designed to mirror the one used on mobile Apple devices (iPhone and iPad) and integrate it with iCloud so that you can store all of your photos in iCloud and then view and manage them on all of your Apple devices.

If you are using the **Photos** app, you can specify how it operates with iCloud in its settings.

1 Open the Photos app and click on **Photos > Settings** on the top toolbar

2 Click on the **General** button to apply settings for items including how Memories are displayed (see page 146), how items are imported, and whether videos and animated photos are played automatically

3 Click on the **iCloud** button for settings for using iCloud with the Photos app

Viewing Photos

The **Photos** app can be used to view photos according to years, months, days or at full size. This enables you to view your photos according to dates and times at which they were taken.

1. Click on the **Library** button in the left-hand sidebar to see the various categories for viewing photos

2. Click on the **All Photos** button on the top toolbar and select options for viewing photos

| Years |
| Months |
| Days |
| ✓ All Photos |

3. For each category – e.g. **Months** – the photos are displayed and collated in easily-accessible formats

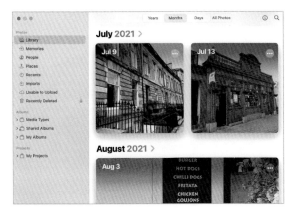

Don't forget

When you first open the Photos app you can select current photo libraries to import. This will ensure that all of the photos you want are available in the **Photos** app when you start.

Hot tip

Photos can be imported into the **Photos** app by selecting **File > Import** from the Menu bar and navigating to the required location within the Finder. This can be used to import photos from your Mac or an external device connected with an USB cable, such as a digital camera, a card reader or a flashdrive.

...cont'd

Don't forget

Drag this slider to change the magnification of the photo(s) being displayed, in **Days** or **All Photos** view:

Hot tip

Click on the **Memories** button in the sidebar to view collections of related photos that have been collated by the Photos app, based on date and the best photos. Double-click on a Memory to view the photos within it. Click on this button in the bottom right-hand corner to view a Memory as a slideshow, with music and themes for transitions between each photo:

4 Double-click on a photo in the **All Photos**, **Days** or **Months** section to view it at full size

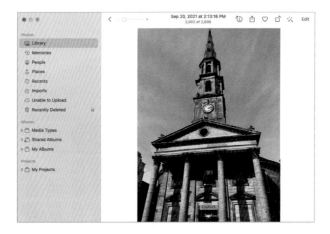

5 For a photo being displayed at full size use these buttons, from left to right, to: view information about it; share the photo; add it as a favorite; rotate it; apply auto-enhancement; and edit it

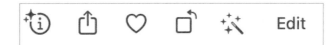

6 Click on the **Memories** button in the left-hand sidebar. This displays photos collated from specific dates (see the Hot tip)

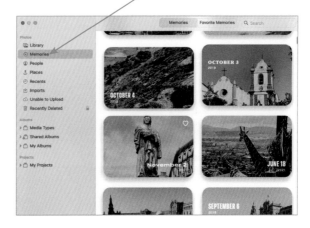

Using the sidebar

In the **Photos** app in macOS, the sidebar at the left-hand side is available regardless of the view being used; e.g. if you are looking at a Memory, or a photo at full size, the sidebar will still be available. To view categories and items in the sidebar:

 Click on a category in the sidebar to view the items in the main window

Click on the **People** or **Places** button in the sidebar to view collections of photos of specific people (based on the results of the Photos app scanning all of the available photos and identifying people within them) or locations where photos have been taken.

The sidebar categories have their own toolbar at the top of the window. For instance, the **Places** category shows locations at which photos have been taken, and this can be viewed in **Map**, **Satellite** or **Grid** format

Editing Photos

The Photos app has a range of editing options that can be used to enhance your photos. To access these options:

1 Open a photo at full size

2 Click on the **Edit** button Edit

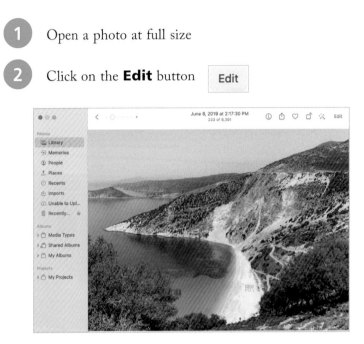

3 The main editing options are accessed from the **Adjust**, **Filters** and **Crop** buttons at the top of the window. Click on one of these to access its options in the right-hand panel

Click on the **Done** button at the top of the Photos app editing window to apply any editing changes that have been made.

4 For the **Adjust** options there is a slider that can be used to apply the amount of the required effect

5 The **Adjust** options also have an **Options** section that can be used to fine-tune the editing effects, such as by dragging the markers at the bottom of the Levels graph

6 Click on the **Filters** button to access preset filters that can be applied to the photo. Click on a filter to view the effect in the photo

Hot tip

In the **Photos** app, Live Photos can also be edited. These are short, animated photos that can be captured on an iPhone or an iPad.

7 Click on the **Crop** button to crop the photo by dragging the corner markers. Drag on the dial to the right of the photo to rotate it

8 Click on the **Done** button to apply the effects

Starting with the Music App

Music is a major part of the Apple ecosystem, and for many years iTunes has been integral to this. However, in macOS Ventura, the iTunes app has been removed and has been replaced with a dedicated Music app. (Other forms of media content – e.g. movies and TV shows – also now have their own dedicated apps – e.g. the TV app or the Podcast app.) To use the Music app:

1 Click on the **Music** app on the Dock

2 Under the **Library** heading in the left-hand sidebar, click on a category to view the available songs; e.g. by **Artists**

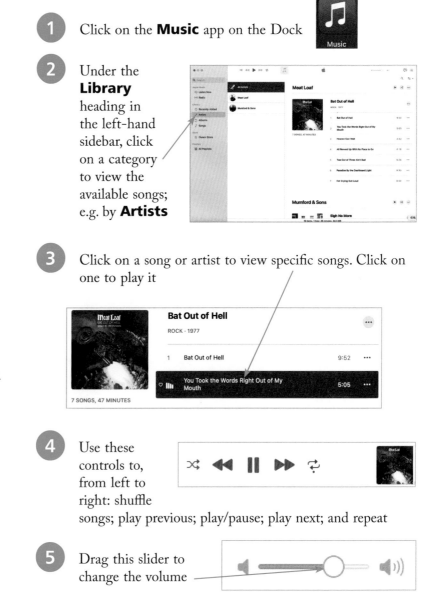

3 Click on a song or artist to view specific songs. Click on one to play it

4 Use these controls to, from left to right: shuffle songs; play previous; play/pause; play next; and repeat

5 Drag this slider to change the volume

Beware

Never import music and use it for commercial purposes as this would be a breach of copyright.

6 Click on the **iTunes Store** button in the left-hand sidebar to access the online store for buying more music

7 Navigate around the iTunes Store Homepage using the panels and sections within the Homepage. Click here to access different music categories

8 Click on a specific artist or album to view the available tracks. Click here to buy a whole album or click on individual songs to buy them

Don't forget

Although iTunes is no longer a separate app in macOS Ventura, the iTunes Store is still available from the Music app. This now just contains music, rather than the variety of content that was previously available in the iTunes Store. Once items have been bought, they are available in the Music app, as shown in Step 2 on the previous page.

151

Beware

Never use illegal music or video download sites. Apart from the legal factor, they are much more likely to contain viruses and spyware.

Using Apple Music

Apple Music is a service that makes the entire Apple Music library of music available to users. It is a subscription service, and music can be streamed over the internet or downloaded so that you can listen to it when you are offline. To start with Apple Music:

Don't forget

Numerous radio stations can also be listened to with Apple Music, including Music 1 (formerly Beats 1).

 Click on the **Music** app on the Dock

 Click on the **Listen Now** button underneath the Apple Music heading in the left-hand sidebar

Hot tip

To cancel your Apple Music subscription at any point, open the App Store app and click on your account icon at the bottom of the left-hand sidebar. Click on the **Account Settings** button at the top of the main window and log in with your Apple ID details. Scroll to the **Manage** section and click on the **Manage** button to access details of your Apple subscriptions. Click on the **Edit** button next to the subscription that you want to cancel and click on the **Cancel Subscription** button.

Click on the **Try It Free** button to select a free three-month trial of the service

Once the free trial has ended, click on one of the subscription options

Apple TV

Apple TV is an online service for downloading movies and TV shows. These were previously accessed from the iTunes app. Content can be bought or rented, depending on the item, and there is also access to the subscription TV service, Apple TV+. The content from Apple TV is accessed from the TV app.

1 Click on the **TV** app on the Dock

2 The initial content is displayed in the **Watch Now** window, with recommended content

3 Use these buttons on the top toolbar to access more content, including **TV+**, **Store** and **Library**

4 Movies and TV shows can be accessed from their relevant categories, and they can be rented or bought. TV+ is a subscription service,

with a free trial. Click on the **Start Free Trial** button to start a seven-day free trial

Hot tip

Apple TV+ can also be accessed from the TV app. This is a monthly subscription service that provides exclusive movies and TV shows, created by Apple.

Hot tip

Click on the **Library** button on the top toolbar to view movies and TV shows that you have downloaded with the TV app.

Don't forget

If you rent a movie from the Apple TV store, you have 30 days to watch it and 48 hours to complete it once you have started watching it.

Podcasts

Podcasts are becoming increasingly widespread and are a popular way to consume a wide range of audio content, covering topics including news, sport and comedy. macOS uses the **Podcasts** app to provide access to a vast library of podcasts.

 Click on the **Podcasts** app on the Dock

Click on the **Browse** button in the left-hand sidebar and swipe up and down to view the available podcasts

Don't forget

Most podcasts consist of regular episodes, usually weekly. Once you have subscribed to a podcast, each episode will be downloaded as it is released. To play a podcast, click on the **Shows** button in the left-hand sidebar and click on the **Play Episode** button.

▶ Play Episode

Click on a podcast to view its details. Click on the + **Follow** button to subscribe to the podcast so that new episodes will be downloaded automatically

Click on these buttons in the left-hand sidebar to access more items in the Podcasts app

Click on these buttons in the left-hand sidebar to view podcasts that you have subscribed to, including the overall show and individual episodes

Reading with Books

Books is an eBook reading app that has been available with Apple's mobile devices, including the iPhone and the iPad, for a number of years. macOS also offers this technology for desktop and laptop Macs. To use Books:

 Click on the **Books** app on the Dock and sign in with your Apple ID

All of the currently-available books are displayed in the **Library**

Don't forget

Items that you have downloaded with Books on other devices will also be available in your Books Library on your Mac, if they are both linked to the same Apple ID.

Click on the **Book Store** heading to view and download more books

Click on a title to preview details about it

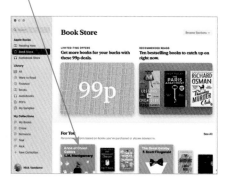

...cont'd

5 Click here to download a book (if it is a paid-for title this button will display a price)

Don't forget

Use these buttons on the top toolbar of a book to, from left to right: view the Table of Contents; view any bookmarks that have been added; or view any notes that you have added:

6 The title will be downloaded into your Books Library. Double-click on the cover to open the book and start reading

Don't forget

Use these buttons on the top toolbar to, from left to right: share a book; change the text size; search for text; and add a bookmark to a page:

7 Click or tap on the right-hand and left-hand edges to turn a page. Move the cursor over the top of the page to access the top toolbar. The bottom toolbar displays the page numbers and location

9 Sharing macOS

This chapter looks at how to set up and manage different user accounts on your Mac.

Adding Users

macOS enables multiple users to access individual accounts on the same computer. If there are multiple users (i.e. two or more for a single machine), each person can log in individually and access their own files and folders. This means that each person can log in to their own settings. All user accounts can be password-protected, to ensure that each user's environment is secure. To set up multiple user accounts:

Don't forget

Every computer with multiple users has at least one main user, also known as the administrator. This means that they have greater control over the number of items that they can edit and alter. If there is only one user on a computer, they automatically take on the role of administrator. Administrators have a particularly important role to play when computers are networked together. Each computer can potentially have several administrators.

1 Click on the **System Settings** icon on the Dock

2 Click on the **Users & Groups** option

 Users & Groups

3 Information about the current user account is displayed. This is your own account, and the information is based on details you provided when you first set up your Mac. Click on the **i** symbol to view more details about an account and apply settings for it

Don't forget

Each user can edit their own icon or photo of themselves, by clicking on the current image and selecting a new option from the available list.

Users & Groups

Nick Vandome Admin	ⓘ
Guest User Off	ⓘ

Add Account...

Automatically log in as	Off ↕
Network account server	Edit...

?

4 Click on the **Add Account...** button to add a new user

Add Account...

5 Enter your Mac password to enable the creation of a new user and click on the **Unlock** button

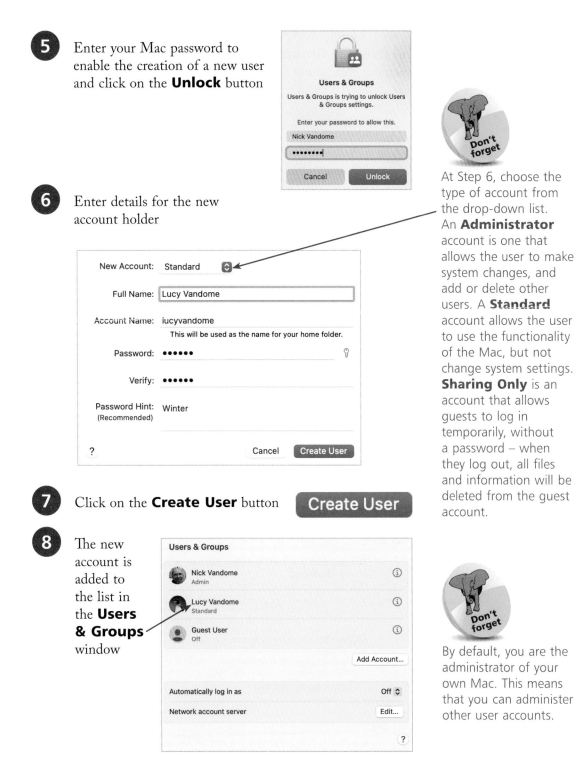

Users & Groups

Users & Groups is trying to unlock Users & Groups settings.

Enter your password to allow this.

Nick Vandome

••••••••

Cancel   Unlock

6 Enter details for the new account holder

New Account:	Standard
Full Name:	Lucy Vandome
Account Name:	iucyvandome
	This will be used as the name for your home folder.
Password:	••••••
Verify:	••••••
Password Hint: (Recommended)	Winter

?   Cancel   Create User

At Step 6, choose the type of account from the drop-down list. An **Administrator** account is one that allows the user to make system changes, and add or delete other users. A **Standard** account allows the user to use the functionality of the Mac, but not change system settings. **Sharing Only** is an account that allows guests to log in temporarily, without a password – when they log out, all files and information will be deleted from the guest account.

7 Click on the **Create User** button   Create User

8 The new account is added to the list in the **Users & Groups** window

Users & Groups

Nick Vandome
Admin   ⓘ

Lucy Vandome
Standard   ⓘ

Guest User
Off   ⓘ

Add Account...

Automatically log in as   Off ⬍

Network account server   Edit...

?

By default, you are the administrator of your own Mac. This means that you can administer other user accounts.

159

Deleting Users

Once a user has been added, their name appears on the list in the **Users & Groups** window (see Step 8 on page 159). It is then possible to edit the details of a particular user or delete them altogether. To do this:

Beware

Always tell other users if you are planning to delete them from the system. Don't just remove them and then let them find out the next time they try to log in. If you delete a user, their personal files are left untouched and can still be accessed, if you select **Don't change the home folder** in Step 3.

160

1 Within **System Settings** > **Users & Groups**, click on the **i** symbol next to the required user account

Lucy Vandome
Standard ⓘ

2 Click on the **Delete Account...** button

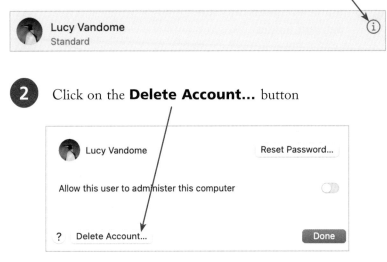

Lucy Vandome   Reset Password...

Allow this user to administer this computer

?   Delete Account...   Done

3 A warning box appears, to check if you really do want to delete the selected user. If you do, select the required option and click on the **Delete Account** button

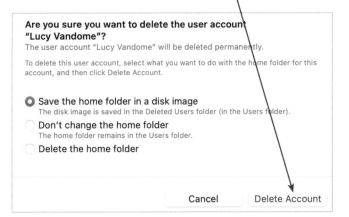

Are you sure you want to delete the user account "Lucy Vandome"?
The user account "Lucy Vandome" will be deleted permanently.

To delete this user account, select what you want to do with the home folder for this account, and then click Delete Account.

○ **Save the home folder in a disk image**
The disk image is saved in the Deleted Users folder (in the Users folder).

○ **Don't change the home folder**
The home folder remains in the Users folder.

○ **Delete the home folder**

Cancel   Delete Account

Fast User Switching

If there are multiple users on your macOS system, it is useful to be able to switch between them as quickly as possible. When this is done, the first user's session is retained so that they can return to it if required. To switch between users:

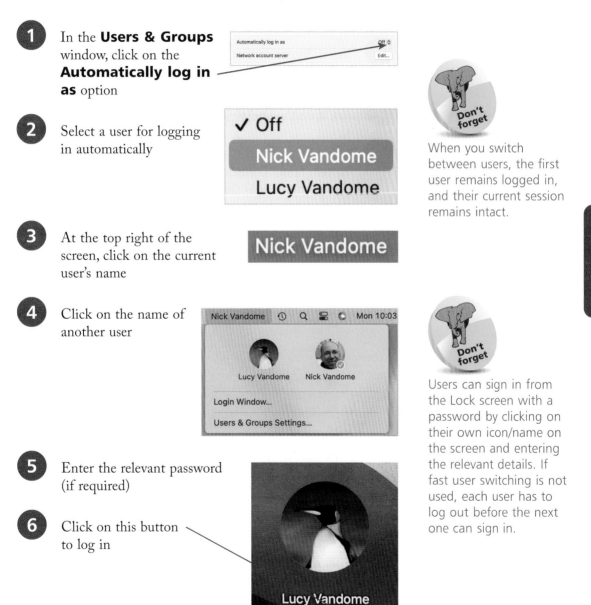

1 In the **Users & Groups** window, click on the **Automatically log in as** option

2 Select a user for logging in automatically

3 At the top right of the screen, click on the current user's name

4 Click on the name of another user

5 Enter the relevant password (if required)

6 Click on this button to log in

Don't forget

When you switch between users, the first user remains logged in, and their current session remains intact.

Don't forget

Users can sign in from the Lock screen with a password by clicking on their own icon/name on the screen and entering the relevant details. If fast user switching is not used, each user has to log out before the next one can sign in.

Screen Time

The amount of time that we spend on our digital devices is a growing issue in society, and steps are being taken to let us see exactly how much time we are spending looking at our computer screens. In macOS, a range of screen-use options can be monitored with the Screen Time feature. To use this:

1 Select **System Settings** > **Screen Time**

 Screen Time

2 Click on the **Options** button

3 Drag the **Screen Time** button **On** to activate Screen Time. The Screen Time options become available once the feature is **On**

Click on the **App Usage** button in the left-hand sidebar to view the overall screen usage.

 App Usage

Screen Time	
⏳ Screen Time	◯
📊 App Usage	>
🔔 Notifications	>
📱 Pickups	>
🕐 Downtime	>
⏳ App Limits	>
👤 Communication Limits	>
✅ Always Allowed	>
🚫 Content & Privacy	>

Share across devices ⬤
You can enable this on any iPhone, iPad, or Mac signed in to iCloud to report your combined screen time.

Use Screen Time Passcode ◯
Use a passcode to secure Screen Time settings, and to allow for more time when limits expire.

Family Sharing Set Up...
Set up Family Sharing to use screen time with your family's devices.

Downtime

This can be used to specify times when the computer and its apps cannot be accessed.

1 Click on the **Every Day** button to apply time limits for a whole week and select the **Custom** option

2 Set time limits for specific days for when items cannot be accessed (only selected apps will be available during Downtime)

App Limits

This can be used to limit the amount of time that certain categories of apps can be accessed.

1 Click on the **Add Limit...** button

2 Click on any category to which you want limits to apply

3 Click here to set a time limit for the categories selected in Step 2. Click on the **Custom** option to apply custom times as for Downtime

In general, the categories for app limits relate to the categories under which the apps are listed in the App Store.

163

...cont'd

Communication Limits

This can be used to specify who can contact you during screen time.

 Communication Limits

1 Click here to select who can contact you during screen time and also downtime, from contacts or everyone

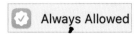

Always Allowed

This can be used to allow the use of specified apps, regardless of other settings.

Always Allowed

1 Drag the buttons **On** for items that you want to allow, regardless of any other Screen Time settings

Content & Privacy

This can be used to add restrictions based on the type of content being viewed.

Content & Privacy

1 Click on the **Content Restrictions** button to restrict content based on criteria such as adult content and explicit language

164

Don't forget

Click on the **Store Restrictions** button under **Content & Privacy** to access options for content that is downloaded from the App Store, the Music app, the TV app and the Podcasts app. Selections can be made for age-appropriate content and also blocking content with explicit language. Click on the **App Restrictions** button to allow the use of specific apps regardless of other privacy restrictions.

10 Networking

This chapter looks at networking and how to share files over a network.

Networking Overview

Before you start sharing files directly between computers, you have to connect them together. This is known as networking and can be done with two computers in the same room, or with thousands of computers in a major corporation. If you are setting up your own small network, it will be known in the computing world as a Local Area Network (LAN). When setting up a network there are various pieces of hardware that are initially required to join all of the network items together. Once this has been done, software settings can be applied for the networked items. Some of the items of hardware that may be required include:

- **A network card**. This is known as a Network Interface Card (NIC), and all recent Macs have them built in.

- **A wireless router**. This is for a wireless network, which is increasingly the most common way to create a network via Wi-Fi. The router is connected to a telephone line and the computer then communicates with it wirelessly.

- **An Ethernet port and Ethernet cable**. This enables you to make a physical connection between devices. Ethernet cables come in a variety of forms, but the one you should be looking for is the Cat6 type as this allows for the fastest transfer of data. If you are creating a wireless network then you will not require these.

- **A hub**. This is a piece of hardware with multiple Ethernet ports that enables you to connect all of your devices together and lets them communicate with each other. However, conflicts can occur with hubs if two devices try to send data through one at the same time.

- **A switch**. This is similar in operation to a hub but it is more sophisticated in its method of data transfer, thus allowing all of the machines on a network to communicate simultaneously, unlike a hub.

Once you have worked out all of the devices that you want to include on your network, you can arrange them accordingly. Try to keep the switches and hub within relative proximity of a power supply, and if you are using cables, make sure they are laid out safely.

Connecting to the internet is also another form of network connection.

The latest models of MacBook do not have a separate Ethernet port. However, a Thunderbolt to Ethernet adapter can be used to connect an Ethernet cable to a MacBook.

Wireless network

The most common method of creating a wireless network is by using Wi-Fi. This involves using a router to connect your Mac computer to the Wi-Fi connection, provided by an external supplier. Once the Wi-Fi connection has been made, the Mac will be able to join compatible online networks: the most common one being the internet. It can also be used to link other computers on a network. The Wi-Fi settings are available within System Settings, in the Wi-Fi section. See page 168 for details about connecting your Mac to a Wi-Fi network.

Another method for connecting items wirelessly is Bluetooth. This covers short distances and is usually used for items such as printers and smartphones. Bluetooth devices can be connected using the **Bluetooth File Exchange** utility: select the required files you want to exchange via Bluetooth and then select the required device.

> **Wi-Fi**
>
> 🛜 Wi-Fi ⬜
>
> ● Wi-Fi is off   Details...
>
> Ask to join networks ⬜
> Known networks will be joined automatically. If no known networks are available, you will have to manually select a network.
>
> Ask to join hotspots 🔵
> Allow this Mac to automatically discover nearby personal hotspots when no Wi-Fi network is available.
>
> Advanced... ?

Ethernet network

Another option for networking computers is to create an Ethernet network. This involves buying an Ethernet hub or switch, which enables you to connect several devices to a central point; i.e. the hub or switch. Older Apple computers and most modern printers have an Ethernet connection, so it is possible to connect various devices, not just computers. Once all of the devices have been connected by Ethernet cables, you can then start applying network settings. If a Mac computer does not have an Ethernet connection, an adapter can be used to connect an Ethernet cable to the Mac.

AirPort network

Apple previously used its own version of Wi-Fi routers to connect to Wi-Fi networks. This was known as AirPort, but was discontinued in 2018. However, these devices can still be used to connect to a Wi-Fi network, although they are no longer supported by Apple.

Network Settings

Once you have connected the hardware needed for a network, you can start applying the network settings that are required for connecting to the internet, for online access.

Beware

When you first connect to your home Wi-Fi network, you will need to enter the passcode for your Wi-Fi router. After this, your Mac will recognize the connection automatically.

1 In **System Settings**, click on the **Network** button

Hot tip

An Ethernet cable can be used to connect to a router, using an adapter (see the second tip on page 166), instead of using a Wi-Fi connection, and it can also be used to connect two computers. For a cable connection, connect an Ethernet cable (via an adapter in the Thunderbolt port) and click on the **Thunderbolt Bridge** option in the Network settings.

2 Click on the **Wi-Fi** option and drag the **Wi-Fi** button **On**

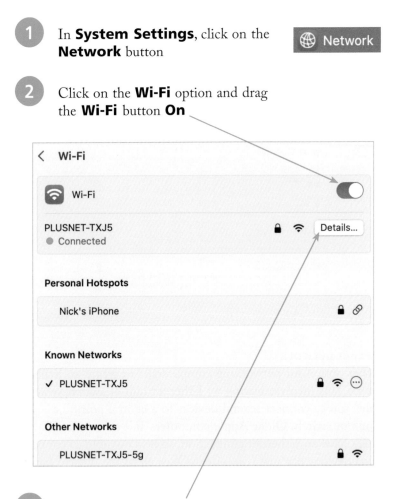

3 Click on the **Details...** button to view the wireless settings for the selected Wi-Fi option

4 Scroll down the page and click on the **Advanced...** button to see the full settings for each option

File Sharing

One of the main reasons for creating a network of two or more computers is to share files between them. On networked Macs, this involves setting them up so that they can share files, and then accessing these files.

Setting up file sharing

To set up file sharing on a networked Mac:

 Click on the **System Settings** app and click on the **General** option

 Click on the **Sharing** option

 Check **On** the boxes next to the items you want to share (the most common items to share are files and printers)

Sharing		
Screen Sharing Off		ⓘ
File Sharing On	⬤	ⓘ
Printer Sharing On	⬤	ⓘ
Remote Login Off		ⓘ
Remote Management Off		ⓘ
Remote Apple Events Off		ⓘ
Internet Sharing Off		ⓘ
Content Caching Off		ⓘ
Media Sharing Off		ⓘ
Bluetooth Sharing On	⬤	ⓘ

Hot tip

For macOS users, files can also be shared with the **AirDrop** option. This can be used with two Macs, and compatible iPhones and iPads that have this facility. Files can be shared simply by dragging them onto the icon of the other user that appears in the AirDrop window. To access AirDrop, click on this button in the Finder:

Connecting to a Network

Connecting as a registered user

To connect as a registered user (usually as yourself when you want to access items on another one of your own computers):

Don't forget

The username and password used to connect to a networked computer as a registered user are the ones used to log in to your Mac. There is also an option to connect using your Apple ID.

Don't forget

You can disconnect from a networked computer by ejecting it in the Finder in the same way as you would for a removable drive, such as a flashdrive (see page 55), by clicking on the **Eject** icon.

1. Click on the **Network** button on the Finder sidebar

2. Click on the networked computer to which you want to connect

3. Click on the **Connect As...** button

4. Check **On** the **Registered User** button, and enter your username and password

5. Click on the **Connect** button

6. The public folders and home folder of the networked computer are available to the registered user. Double-click on an item to view its contents

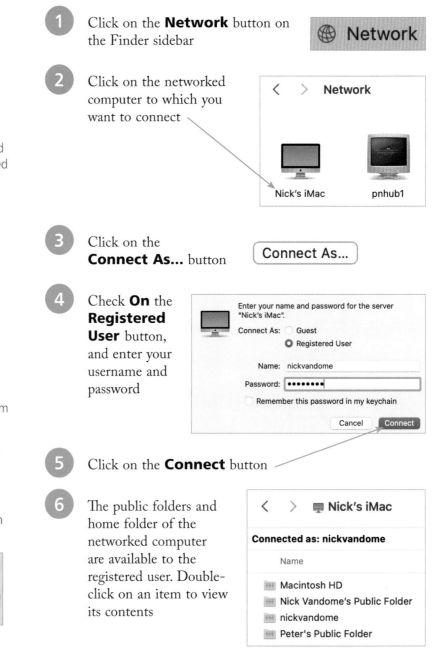

...cont'd

Guest users

Guest users on a network are users other than yourself or other registered users, to whom you want to limit access to your files and folders. Guests only have access to a folder called Drop Box in your own Public folder. To share files with guest users you have to first copy them into the Drop Box folder. To do this:

1. Create a file and select **File > Save** from the Menu bar

2. Navigate to your own Home folder (this is created automatically by macOS and displayed in the Finder sidebar with your Mac username)

3. Double-click on the **Public** folder

4. Double-click on the **Drop Box** folder

5. Save the file into the Drop Box folder

Beware

If another user is having problems accessing the files in your Drop Box folder, check the permissions settings that have been assigned to the files. See page 186 for further details.

Hot tip

The contents of the Drop Box folder can be accessed by other users on the same computer as well as users on the network.

Beware

The Drop Box folder is not the same as the Dropbox app, which is used for online storage and backing up.

171

...cont'd

Accessing a Drop Box folder
To access files in a Drop Box folder:

Beware

It is better to copy files into the Drop Box folder rather than moving them completely from their primary location.

Hot tip

Set permissions for how the Drop Box folder operates by selecting it in the Finder and **Ctrl** + **clicking** on it. Select **Get Info** from the menu, and apply the required settings under the **Sharing & Permissions** heading.

1 Access a networked computer as shown on page 170

2 Click on the **Connect As...** button in the Finder window

3 Check **On** the **Guest** button

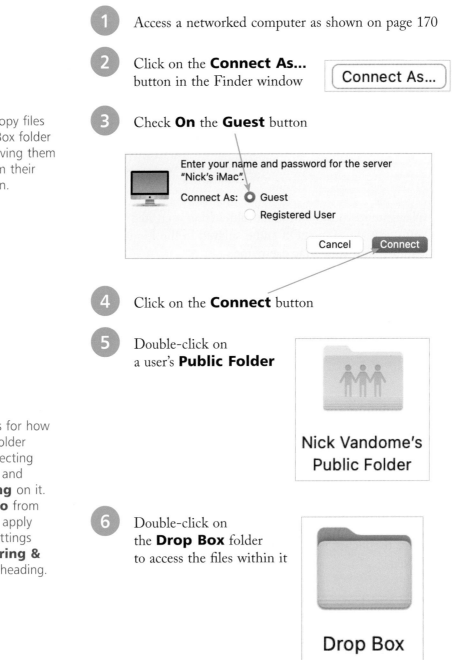

4 Click on the **Connect** button

5 Double-click on a user's **Public Folder**

Nick Vandome's Public Folder

6 Double-click on the **Drop Box** folder to access the files within it

Drop Box

11 Maintaining macOS

Despite its stability, macOS still benefits from a robust maintenance regime. This chapter looks at ways to keep macOS in top shape and ensure apps are as secure as possible, and looks at some general troubleshooting.

Time Machine

Time Machine is a feature of macOS that gives you great peace of mind. In conjunction with an external hard drive it creates a backup of your whole system, including folders, files, apps, and even the macOS operating system itself.

Once it has been set up, Time Machine takes a backup every hour, and you can then go into Time Machine to restore any files that have been deleted or become corrupt since the last backup.

Setting up Time Machine

To use Time Machine, it first has to be set up. This involves attaching a hard drive to your Mac via cable or wirelessly, depending on the type of hard drive you have. To set up Time Machine:

Beware

Make sure that you have an external hard drive that is larger than the contents of your Mac, otherwise Time Machine will not be able to back it all up.

Don't forget

The hard drive must be connected in order to use Time Machine.

1 Click on the **Time Machine** option in **System Settings** > **General**

Time Machine

2 In the Time Machine window, click on the **Add Backup Disk...** button

< Time Machine

Time Machine
Time Machine backs up your computer and keeps local snapshots and hourly backups for the past 24 hours, daily backups for the past month and weekly backups for all previous months. The oldest backups and any local snapshots are deleted as space is needed.

Add Backup Disk...   ?

3 In the Time Machine window, click on the **Set Up Disk...** button

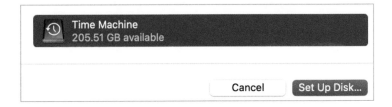

Time Machine
205.51 GB available

Cancel   Set Up Disk...

4 Connect an external hard drive and select it from the list

5 The backup will begin. The initial backup copies your whole system and can take several hours. Subsequent hourly backups only look at items that have been changed since the previous backup. Details of the latest backup, and when the next one is due, are shown here

6 Click on the **Options...** button for settings that can be applied for the Time Machine backup process

When you first set up Time Machine it copies everything on your Mac. Depending on the type of connection you have for your external drive, this could take several hours. Because of this, it is a good idea to have a hard drive with a USB 3.0 or Thunderbolt connection to make it as fast as possible.

If you stop the initial backup before it has been completed, Time Machine will remember where it has stopped and resume the backup from this point.

175

...cont'd

Using Time Machine

Once Time Machine has been set up, it can then be used to go back in time to view items in an earlier state. To do this:

1 Access an item on your Mac and delete it. In this example, the **Time Machine 1** folder has been deleted

2 Click on the **Time Machine** icon on the Dock or in the Launchpad

3 Time Machine displays the selected window in its current state (the **Time Machine 1** folder is deleted). Earlier versions are stacked behind it

4 Click on the arrows to move through the open items, or select a time or date from the scale to the right of the arrows

5 Another way to move through Time Machine is to click on the pages behind the first one. This brings the selected item to the front

6   Move back through the windows
to find the deleted item. Click on it
and click on the **Restore** button to restore the item, in
this case the **Time Machine 1** folder

Items are restored
from the Time Machine
backup disk; i.e. the
external hard drive.

7   Click on the **Cancel** button to return
to your normal environment, without
restoring the item

8   The deleted **Time Machine 1** folder is now
restored to its original location

Disk Utility

Disk Utility is a utility app that allows you to perform certain testing and repair functions for macOS. It incorporates a variety of functions, and is a good option for both general maintenance and if your computer is not running as it should.

Each of the functions within Disk Utility can be applied to specific drives and volumes. However, it is not possible to use the macOS start-up disk within Disk Utility as this will be in operation to run the app, and Disk Utility cannot operate on a disk that has apps already running. To use Disk Utility:

Checking disks

Disk Utility is located within the **Applications > Utilities (Other)** folder.

1 Open Disk Utility then click the **First Aid** tab to check a disk

2 Select a disk and select one of the **First Aid** options

Erasing a disk
To erase all of the data on a disk or a volume:

If there is a problem with a disk and macOS can fix it, the **Repair** button will be available. Click on this to enable Disk Utility to repair the problem.

1 Click on the **Erase** tab, and select a disk or a volume

If you erase data from a removable disk such as a flashdrive, you will not be able to retrieve it.

2 Click **Erase** to erase the data on the selected disk or volume

Erase

178

System Information

This can be used to view how the different hardware and software elements on your Mac are performing. To do this:

 Open the **Utilities** folder and double-click on the **System Information** icon

 Click on the **Hardware** link and click on an item of hardware

System Information is located within the **Applications > Utilities (Other)** folder.

 Details about the item of hardware, and its performance, are displayed

Intel Iris Plus Graphics 640:

Chipset Model:	Intel Iris Plus Graphics 640
Type:	GPU
Bus:	Built-In
VRAM (Dynamic, Max):	1536 MB
Vendor:	Intel
Device ID:	0x5926
Revision ID:	0x0006
Metal:	Supported, feature set macOS GPUFamily2 v1
Metal Family:	Supported, Metal GPUFamily macOS 2
Displays:	

Color LCD:

Display Type:	Built-In Retina LCD
Resolution:	2560 x 1600 Retina
Framebuffer Depth:	24-Bit Color (ARGB8888)
Main Display:	Yes
Mirror:	Off
Online:	Yes
Automatically Adjust Brightness:	Yes
Connection Type:	Internal

 Similarly, click on network or software items to view their details

Activity Monitor

Activity Monitor is a utility app that can be used to view information about how much processing power and memory is being used to run apps. This can be useful to know if certain apps are running slowly or crashing frequently. To use Activity Monitor:

Don't forget

Activity Monitor is located within the **Applications > Utilities (Other)** folder.

Activity Monitor

 Open Activity Monitor and click on the **CPU** tab to see how much processor capacity is being used up

System:	3.12%	CPU LOAD	Threads:	1,990
User:	3.94%		Processes:	594
Idle:	92.94%			

2 Click on the **Memory** tab to see how much system memory (RAM) is being used up

MEMORY PRESSURE	Physical Memory:	8.00 GB	App Memory:	3.20 GB
	Memory Used:	6.41 GB	Wired Memory:	2.09 GB
	Cached Files:	1.48 GB	Compressed:	1.13 GB
	Swap Used:	2.34 GB		

3 Click on the **Energy** tab to see details of battery usage (for a laptop)

ENERGY IMPACT			BATTERY (Last 12 hours)
	Remaining charge:	31%	
	Time remaining:	1:58	
	Time on battery:	65:10	

 Click on the **Disk** tab to see how much space has been taken up on the hard drive

Reads in:	6,387,496	IO ⌄	Data read:	193.32 GB
Writes out:	3,117,316		Data written:	121.86 GB
Reads in/sec:	0		Data read/sec:	819 bytes
Writes out/sec:	34		Data written/sec:	207 KB

Updating Software

Apple periodically releases updates for its software; both its apps and the macOS operating system. All of these are now available through the App Store. To update software:

1 Open **System Settings** > **General** and click on the **Software Update** option

2 All available updates, if any, will be displayed. Click on the **Update Now** button to install them. If your macOS is up-to-date, this will be noted. Click on the **i** symbol to apply settings for how updates are installed

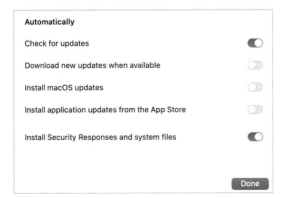

3 Make the relevant selections for how updates are managed, including checking for them automatically and downloading new updates when they are available. Click on the **Done** button to confirm any changes

Don't forget

For some software updates, such as those for the macOS itself, you may have to restart your computer for them to take effect.

Security

Internet security is an important issue for every computer user; no-one wants their computer to be infected with a virus or malicious software. Historically, Macs have been less prone to attack from viruses than Windows-based machines, but this does not mean Mac users can be complacent. With their increasing popularity there is now more temptation for virus writers to target them. macOS recognizes this, and has taken steps to prevent attacks with the Security function. To use this:

1 Open **System Settings** and click on the **Privacy & Security** option

 Privacy & Security

2 Scroll up the page to the **Security** section. Click on one of the buttons at the top of the page to determine which location apps can be downloaded from. You can select from just **App Store** or **App Store and identified developers**, which gives you added security in terms of apps having been thoroughly checked

Beware

The other option in the Security section is for **Lockdown Mode**. However, this should only be used if you think your Mac has been subjected to a sophisticated cyberattack. If this happens it is best to take your Mac to a computer security specialist.

3 Click on the **Turn On...** button for the **FileVault** option to encrypt the data on your Mac, for added security for your files

Privacy

Also within the System Settings are options for activating a firewall and privacy settings. To access these:

Activating a firewall
A firewall can be used to prevent malicious software gaining access to your Mac via your Wi-Fi connection. To do this:

 Access **System Settings > Network** and click on the **Firewall** option

 Drag the **Firewall** button **On**

Privacy settings
To apply privacy settings for specific apps:

1 Access **System Settings > Privacy & Security**

2 Under the **Privacy** heading, click on the **Location Services** option to select apps that can be used to determine the location of your Mac

Privacy & Security

Privacy

◢ Location Services		>
▨ Contacts		>
🗓 Calendars		>

3 Click on specific listed apps to view other apps that have requested access to them. Grant or deny this access as required. For instance, you may want to limit access to your own personal files and folders

Don't forget

For options for specific apps in Step 3, drag the buttons **On** or **Off** to grant or deny access for that option.

Problems with Apps

The simple answer

macOS is something of a rarity in the world of computing software: it claims to be remarkably stable, and it is. However, this is not to say that things do not sometimes go wrong, although this is considerably less frequent than with older Mac operating systems. Sometimes this will be due to problems within particular apps, and on occasion the problems may lie with macOS itself. If this does happen, the first course of action is to restart macOS using the **Apple menu** > **Restart** command. If this does not work, or you cannot access the **Restart** command as the Mac has frozen, try turning off the power to the computer and then starting up again.

Force quitting

If a particular app is not responding, it can be closed down separately without the need to reboot the computer. To do this:

Beware

When there are updates to macOS, these can on rare occasions cause issues with some apps. However, these are usually fixed with subsequent patches and upgrades to macOS.

 Select **Apple menu** > **Force Quit...** from the Menu bar

 Select the app you want to close

 Click the **Force Quit** button

General Troubleshooting

It is true that things do occasionally go wrong with macOS, although probably with less regularity than with some other operating systems. If something does go wrong, there are a number of areas that you can check and also some steps you can take to ensure that you do not lose any important data if the worst-case scenario occurs, and your hard drive packs up completely:

- **Backup**. If everything does go wrong it is essential that you have taken preventative action in the form of making sure that all of your data is backed up and saved. This can be done with either the Time Machine app or by backing up manually by copying data to a flashdrive. Some content is also automatically backed up if you have iCloud activated.

- **Reboot**. One traditional reply by IT helpdesks is to reboot (i.e. turn off the computer and turn it back on again) and hope that the problem has resolved itself. In a lot of cases this simple operation does the trick, but it is not always a viable solution for major problems.

- **Check cables**. If the problem appears to be with a network connection or an externally-connected device, check that all cables are connected properly and have not become loose. If possible, make sure that all cables are tucked away so that they cannot be inadvertently pulled out.

- **Check network settings**. If your network or internet connections are not working, check the network settings in System Settings. Sometimes when you make a change to one item, this can have an adverse effect on one of these settings.

- **Check for viruses**. If your computer is infected with a virus, this could affect the efficient running of the machine. Luckily, this is less of a problem for Macs as virus writers tend to concentrate their efforts toward Windows-based machines. However, this is changing as Macs become more popular, and there are plenty of Mac viruses out there. So, make sure your computer is protected by an app such as Norton AntiVirus, which is available from **www.norton.com**

In extreme cases, you will not be able to reboot your computer normally. If this happens, you will have to pull out the power cable and re-attach it. You will then be able to reboot, although the computer may want to check its hard drive to make sure that everything is in working order.

...cont'd

Beware

If you are having problems opening a document that you have been sent from a trusted source, contact them to make sure that the document has not been locked with a password. If you receive documents from someone you do not know, such as by email, do not open them as they may contain viruses or malware.

- **Check start-up items**. If you have set certain items to start automatically when your computer is turned on, this could cause certain conflicts within your machine. If this is the case, disable the items from launching during the booting-up of the computer. This can be done within the **General** section of **System Settings** by clicking on the **Login Items** option and adding or deleting options in the **Open at Login** panel at the top of the window.

- **Check permissions**. If you or other users are having problems opening items, this could be because of the permissions that are set. To check these, select the item in the Finder, click on the **File** button on the top Menu bar and select **Get Info**. In the **Sharing & Permissions** section of the **Info** window you will be able to set the relevant permissions to allow other users, or yourself, to read, write or have no access.

Click here to view permissions settings

- **Eject external devices**. Sometimes external devices, such as flashdrives, can become temperamental and refuse to eject the disks within them, or even not show up on the Desktop or in the Finder at all. If this happens, you can try to eject the disk by pressing the mouse button when the Mac chimes are heard during the booting-up process.

- **Turn off your screen saver**. Screen savers can sometimes cause conflicts within your computer, particularly if they have been downloaded from an unreliable source. If this happens, change the screen saver within the **Screen Saver** section of **System Settings**, or disable it altogether.

Index